Divine F )

Unity beyond Duality

*Living a life of love, commitment
and energetic interconnectedness*

Nicholas C. Demetry, M.D.

Copyright 2010 Nicholas C. Demetry, M.D.
All Rights Reserved
No part of this book may be reproduced, stored in a
retrieval system, or transmitted by any means,
electronic, mechanical, photocopying, recording, or
otherwise without written permission from the author.

ISBN13: 978-0-9792961-1-6
ISBN 10: 0-9792961-1-0

Editing
Diane Kistner, DD, MSW
Shared Road Productions
info@sharedroads.net

Book Design
Donna Overall
donnaoverall@bellsouth.net

Original Graphics & Diagrams
Donna Overall
donnaoverall@bellsouth.net

**ETHERIKOS
PRESS**

www.etherikos.com

Table of Contents

About the Author

Nicholas Demetry, M.D., is a holistic psychiatrist. He received his medical degree from Emory University School of Medicine. After completing his medical training, he continued his studies at the University of Hawaii, specializing in general psychiatry and transcultural studies.

Dr. Demetry is Director of the Etherikos International School of Energy Healing and Spiritual Development headquartered in Atlanta, Georgia. The school has offered programs and classes in the United States and more than a dozen other countries. He is Director of the Institute for Spiritual Health, a non-profit organization which promotes peace through spiritual health and education, and is also a Founding Diplomate of the American Board of Holistic Medicine. Dr. Demetry is currently in private practice in Atlanta.

Acknowledgments

My deepest gratitude and love go first to my wife, Maria, for walking the path of marriage that we share together; for her care, laughter, and impecccable neutrality in the face of life's challenges; for believing in me; and for making space for my soul to follow the path of heart and service that we share.

Special thanks go to Diane Kistner for her creative guidance and masterful editing of the manuscript and to Donna Overall for her tireless efforts and inspired input into the graphics.

My love and gratitude go out to my grandparents, Anna and Nick; to my great uncle and aunt, Pota and Charlie; to my parents for bringing me into the world; and to my mother, Chrysanthy, and stepfather, Demetrius, who married in their late seventies and shared 17 beautiful years, setting the example for all of us that it's never too late to love again.

Finally, my gratitude and love go out to all of our couple-friends who walk the shared path of heart and spiritual service to the world: Guy and Marie, Jerry and Beverly, Jack and Bea, Fatima and Willie, John and Michelle, Eva and Rudi, Krista and Attila, Joachim and Anna-Marie, Sam and Nilou, Hartmut and Olga, Martina and Ladislav, Kristina and Milda, Olga and Dushan, and many, many more.

On Marriage

You were born together, and together you shall be forevermore.
You shall be together when the white wings of death scatter your days.
Yes, you shall be together even in the silent memory of God.
But let there be spaces in your togetherness,
And let the winds of the heavens dance between you.

Love one another, but make not a bond of love:
Let it rather be a moving sea between the shores of your souls.
Fill each other's cup but drink not from one cup.
Give one another of your bread but eat not from the same loaf
Sing and dance together and be joyous, but let each one of you be alone,
Even as the strings of a lute are alone though they quiver with the same music.

Give your hearts, but not into each other's keeping.
For only the hand of Life can contain your hearts.
And stand together yet not too near together:
For the pillars of the temple stand apart,
And the oak tree and the cypress grow not in each other's shadow.

– Kahlil Gibran, *The Prophet*

Introduction

THIS BOOK IS ABOUT the nature of relationship, your relationship to the outer world—to other people and your partner—but also how you relate within yourself to your own inner male and female energies. Whole books (and even entire bodies of work) have been devoted to exploring one or more aspects of relationship dynamics. The goal of this book is to synthesize some of these teachings[1] into an essential, core approach, then build from that core a meta-framework to help you evolve and spiritually deepen your relationship with yourself and with your partner.

You are encouraged to refer periodically to the master diagram that appears on the back cover. A larger version is included in the last pages of this book. This diagram is a simplified visualization of the complex, multidimensional spiraling of energies we experience in divine partnership. Clarifying graphical representations of portions of this master diagram are presented in the text as various concepts are introduced and discussed. Taken together, they represent how human relationships evolve through physical, emotional, mental, and spiritual dimensions—a divine alchemical process that ultimately leads to divine union and wholeness.

We will begin with the basic energy polarities of female and male, referred to in Chinese thought as *yin* and *yang*, and what constitutes healthy and unhealthy male and female energies. We will then touch on developmental woundings that can propel us into unhealthy relationships, especially the codependent triangle—a powerful developmental binding and blending of energies arising from the parent–child relationship that is actually evolutionary but can become solidified and dysfunctional, a prison of the soul. The remainder of the book provides a way out of this prison, including steps to achieving a transformed state of divine love in partnership.

---

[1] *See the annotated bibliography for source material and commentary.*

The concepts and skills presented in this book will help you achieve a dynamic balance of healthy male and female energies in your relationship with your partner and within yourself. Working together, you will set in motion the alchemical process that leads to divine partnership.

As important core concepts are presented and elaborated in this book, you are encouraged to refer back to the master diagram to integrate the presented materials into the portion of the meta-framework they represent.[2] By taking the time to do this, you will be able to deeply explore the complexities of human relationship from a point of essential clarity and wisdom.

---

[2] *Note that some of this material is quite advanced. To avoid confusion, some concepts may be introduced only briefly in this book.*

Male and Female Energies in Partnership

IF WE SPEAK about male and female, female and male, we don't just think of women and men. We think of feminine and masculine qualities—of *yin* and *yang*, of *anima* and *animus*. In essence, these are energy polarities. Before I cover how male and female energies are expressed in partnership, it will be helpful to anchor the core concept in a simple visual way:

Note the minus and plus signs corresponding, respectively, to the female and male poles. I want to emphasize that these are not the same as negative and positive, unhealthy or healthy. We can think of these polarities as being similar to a magnet with negative and positive poles. One pole is not better than the other; each polarity is an essential aspect of the magnet itself, and each is equally powerful. Please keep this distinction in mind as we proceed.

It will also be helpful to keep in mind that your ability to understand and work with complex ideas begins with being clear about a few simple concepts. I'll give you an example. When you were conceived, you inherited half of your genes from your father and half from your mother: ½ + ½ = 1. Even at the basic physical level—not to mention the emotional, mental, and spiritual levels—how those genes intermingle and are expressed as the new being that you are and are becoming can be bewilderingly complex; if you get confused, it helps to refer back to the core concept: ½ + ½ = 1. And so it is with the female–male polarities.

Energies can be thought of as working somewhat like genes do. As I discuss the qualities of male and female energy, ask yourself: *What were my parents like? What about the way they expressed themselves and how they behaved was healthy or unhealthy?* Because the first projections of the male–female dynamic that we receive and assimilate come from our parents, you can see which of their qualities you are holding that keep you from moving on to a better way of relating to your partner. Keep in mind that it is not always the father who expresses the male energy; a mother can be expressing male energy also. We will talk about this in more detail later.

Qualities of Male–Female Energy

The male and female polarities each consist of four qualities of unhealthy and healthy energy. First let's look at the qualities of male energy.

Unhealthy male energy

1. alienation
2. domination
3. fear of relationships and commitment
4. a drive to destroy

Healthy male energy

1. autonomy
2. strength
3. self-sufficiency
4. constructive power

If you think of the world today, can you identify the unhealthy male energy? It's easy. Just look at the way our societies now operate and ask yourself if it's healthy or dysfunctional. You can see that many societal functions are not really working. Gridlock prevails. Businesses and governmental agencies have taken charge of functions that used to be handled by the family, such as growing and processing food, preparing meals, childcare, and education.

What about unhealthy female energy? As with the masculine qualities, there are four qualities of unhealthy and healthy female energy.

Unhealthy female energy

1. lost in relationship (helpless)
2. being dominated (submissive)
3. fused (as opposed to connected) with the other
4. tending to panic

Healthy female energy

1. flowing
2. socially oriented
3. caring, nurturing
4. compassionate

If the female energy is being stressed and not responding in a healthy way, then it cannot flow freely; it can become chaotic, confused, hysterical, and helpless. If the male energy is being stressed, it also cannot flow freely; it can become noncommittal, alienating, domineering, and destructive. Can you think of what happens to you when you are stressed? Which of the unhealthy male and female qualities do you take on when you get really stressed? Now ask yourself, *Where did I learn this?*

When you find an inner balance between your male and female energies, then the four healthy qualities of each side are expressed. The male side expresses autonomy, strength, independence or self-sufficiency, and freedom. The female side becomes flowing, socially oriented, nurturing, caring, and compassionate.

Often people grow up witnessing examples of both healthy and unhealthy energies from both of their parents. For example, a mother can express healthy female or healthy male energies while the father is expressing unhealthy energies, or vice versa. We internalize these qualities into ourselves. So, for example, some women have a more developed healthy male energy within themselves than they do female energy. On the other hand, the opposite can happen: A man can have a healthy connection to his female side but not to his male side; maybe he had a loving, nurturing mother but an unhealthy father figure. Sometimes we'll see a healthy male and female figure in one parent and unhealthy counterparts in the other.

So think about this: If you take the unbalanced energies of your parents into yourself, what are you likely to attract into your life? You can attract the same kind of energy, because you are familiar with it even though you are not happy with it. On the other hand, it can happen that you attract totally the opposite energy with the new problem that a partner expresses the healthy energy, but you took on unhealthy energy as a child and might still express that unhealthy energy in your relationship, especially when you are stressed.

Let's return to the basic male and female energy polarities, presented in a more dynamic way.

Yin and Yang

From an Eastern perspective, we can think of male and female energies in terms of the complementary qualities of *yin* and *yang* as represented in the well known yin–yang symbol of Taoism:

Normally *yang*, depicted in the symbol as white, is considered the active, masculine side; *yin*, in black, is the receptive, passive, feminine side. In Chinese thought, naturally occurring dualities—such as dark and light, female and male—are considered manifestations of *yin* and *yang*. These qualities are not static. All things have both *yin* and *yang* aspects that interact constantly, as indicated by the small amount of *yin* embodied within the *yang* and the small amount of *yang* embodied within the *yin*. These complementary embodiments are akin to Carl Jung's psychological concepts of the *anima* (the feminine) in men and the *animus* (the masculine) in women. *Yang* and *yin* energies are at work in the alchemical process that leads to divine partnership.

As we did with the qualities of energy in the male and female, let's now look at the qualities and activities of the masculine *yang* and feminine *yin* energies.

Yang energy

- left brain dominance
- focused on outer realities
- problem-solving
- very concrete activities (building, repairing, etc.)
- reason
- intellect
- being abstract
- analysis
- thoughts
- objectivity
- duty
- will
- work
- service
- asceticism
- *animus*

Also we can think of *yang* as the elements of fire and air, which are rather masculine.

Yin energy

- right brain dominance
- focused on inner realities
- subjectivity
- emotions
- intuition
- imagination
- receptivity
- sensuality
- play
- art
- *anima*

We can also think of *yin* as the elements of earth and water, which are more feminine.

Religions over the ages have suggested two valid spiritual paths. One path, dedicating one's life to asceticism, we could say involves transmuting matter into spirit or energy, which involves elements of fire and air. This path is more *yang*. The other path is having a physical relationship through a family, transmuting energy into matter, and this is the *yin* approach involving elements of earth and water. Either path, the *yin* or the *yang*, is an authentic way to get to know who you really are. A person may choose to pursue one path or the other at different times in life.

Male energy approaches things differently from female energy. For example, a man's reasoning process follows along a straight line, which is a feature of left brain dominance:

A woman's reasoning process tends to be more like this:

This kind of thinking is a feature of right brain dominance, or whole-brain thinking, which is also expressed in the fact that women are more relationship-oriented.

Let's look at some examples of how *yang* and *yin* energies and aspects operate. Take the classic example of going to a party. The wife may be very happy to go to the party, while her husband is reluctant to go. When the couple gets to the party, all the women go into the kitchen. They begin to talk sociably, focused on being at the party, and they have a good time. The men watch their watches. They orient their conversation toward work or sports events or TV. They talk about something that they have done or achieved or the state of the world in general—anything but being at the party.

When it comes to the theme of justice—what is right and what is wrong in a situation—male energy tends to define right and wrong and follow what is thought to be justice. Men are often very justice-oriented: "You made a mistake; pay for it." They are very straight-thinking. Female thinking about justice is more like "It's not good that they did that, but you have to have a little compassion and understanding." Female energy is concerned about what the other person was thinking as well as the impact of their behavior: "It's okay, let it go, let it go." Male thinking is more like "If I don't get justice on this, I can't rest. I've got to do it and finish it. I have to finish the job." Female thinking is very relationship-oriented. Women tend more toward involvement with others and partnership. Men tend to isolate more and step back. These are traditional male–female energies.

This is about more than just the relationship between two people. As shown in the master diagram, and as we'll discuss in more detail later, much more is going on. For now, know that a transformative process is involved, a process we can think of as divine alchemy. The ultimate goal of this process is to achieve wholeness: to balance the *yang* and *yin* sides, to develop both male and female aspects within the self, and to more consciously develop the spiritual union of male and female energies in relationship.

So let's look at how the process begins. Whether male or female, depending on the qualities we are born with, we start out on one track or the other. Some women, for example, come into life with a more developed *yang* side instead of the more typically feminine *yin*. The same is true with men who have a more developed *yin* side than *yang*. Your development is influenced by your environment—especially how your parents parented you. Sometimes in a family, the mother has a more masculine energy, and vice versa for the father. If the energy polarities were reversed in your parents, that is what you have experienced and internalized in some way.

Something very interesting is happening in the world now. Even though there are still very traditional societies where the male–female polarities are very clear and defined, this is changing very rapidly. Some polarity issues have developed in the last forty or fifty years in the technologically developed countries. Consider the feminist movement and how many women moved toward careers and working outside of the home. There was a substantial shift in energy as women developed their more masculine side. This shift created a conflict for men. Many men struggled against it, but many more began to shift more into their feminine side. Then that energy shift became an issue for women. Because clear new roles for men and women have not yet been defined, many people have become much more conscious of energy polarities and where they stand in their development.

As difficult as these energy shifts have been, they are helping make us aware of the importance of balancing our male and female energies. If you are a woman and you are shifted too much to the male polarity, you are missing something in yourself. If you are a man and you are too female-polarized, you are missing something in yourself.

With the polarity balancing process we are going through, a sort of transformational merging is taking place, and this is what I'll refer to as divine alchemy. Whether you occupy a female body or a male body, bringing your female and male energies, your *yin* and *yang,* into balance is the nature of wholeness. Ultimately, it is likely that divine alchemy will bring humanity as a whole into greater balance. This is really the evolutionary goal.

Wounding and Its Effect on Partnership

WE FIRST LEARN about partnership as children being raised by our parents or other parental figures. Even in the best of circumstances, we all experience wounding as children that affects the way we feel about ourselves and how we relate to others as adults. As we grow up within a family, we adopt or strain against roles we see modeled for us by the adults who take care of us. This results in enduring patterns of relating that we often are not even conscious of. Let's look at some ways love is expressed in healthy ways and how we can be wounded if love is withheld or expressed in unhealthy ways.

Expressions of Love and Wounding

Love is essential for healthy development, and it is what divine partnership is all about. We first experience love within our family of origin. According to Gary Chapman in *The Five Love Languages of Children*, love is expressed in five ways:

1. Physical touch and affection
2. Words of affirmation and kindness
3. Quality time spent together
4. Acts of service and education
5. Gifts, sharing, and giving

If children witness and experience healthy expressions of love, they develop the ability to receive and give love in a healthy way. They develop the capacity for divine love. If, however, love is modeled for them in unhealthy ways—or is not expressed at all—children do not learn how to express love in healthy ways. They become wounded, and they often carry the wounds with them all their lives. They grow up not really understanding how to love themselves, much less how to express love in healthy ways to their own children or their partners.

The very idea of "divine love" is hard for them to grasp, and this may constrain their spiritual development as well. Some lose touch with their own soul.

To have healthy relationships, those who were wounded in childhood—and that is many of us—must learn to experience as adults the love they did not experience as children. Let's look now at the five ways of expressing love.

Physical touch and affection

The first avenue for expressing love, *physical touch,* involves appropriate affectionate touching, hugging, massage, and tickling. Physical touch is a vehicle through which healthy, divine love can be transmitted, but touch can be misused. If touch is expressed in a loving, healthy way, then the child feels recognized and validated. But if touch means being hit and punished or is otherwise used as a way to gratify a parent at the child's expense, then it is not an expression of love; it is abuse. Abuse teaches the child to express love in unhealthy ways. Withholding touch, which is considered neglect, is a failure to model love. Why does this poor modeling happen? Often the parents still carry a similar wounding from their own childhoods. Wounded, they are not able to touch affectionately, so the child is deprived of physical contact and feels neglected and unloved.

Words of affirmation and kindness

The second way love is expressed is through *words of kindness,* which can be in the form of affirmations like "You did a good job. I love you. You are so beautiful, so wonderful. You are great." This allows the soul of a child to continue feeling a connectedness to love through the parents. Without this sense of connectedness, the child's soul will feel unsafe in the world and—as we'll see when we discuss codependency—the child will adopt a constrained, defensive position. So, how can words be used to abuse or misuse? Maybe the child is judged or criticized through words (and maybe also hit, which is a double wounding). Or the parents are always screaming at or talking too loudly to the child. As with physical touch, words can also be withheld and love not expressed. If a child is never heard or talked to with love and attention, the child has no idea what the parents really feel. The adults may never ask what the child needs or wants or show respect for the child's wishes, needs, or desires. Yet another possibility is that words are shared but the parent's body language and feelings contradict the words. The child may hear "I love you" but see an angry face.

In such situations, the soul of the child doesn't feel that it can remain present in the world. It has to withdraw behind a defense, like the body scars over to protect a wound. Even though the soul is our most powerful and eternal self, it is in enemy territory in the physical world. The soul can be encouraged by love to remain present, to grow, and to flourish. But, in the absence of love or in the presence of twisted and wounded love, the soul withdraws. When this happens, the heart shuts down and the ego, will, and intellect take its place. This creates ego patterns that are incapable of expressing authentic feelings. These patterns are really scars. They are masks—what psychologists call false selves—and they are related to what we refer to as elementals: charged thought–emotion complexes or emotion–thought complexes that are stored in our energy body.

Quality time spent together

The third way a parent can express love for a child and keep the soul's presence open is by *spending quality time* with the child, engaging in activities that are meaningful for the child—not just at the parent's convenience, but when the child needs the attention and they are doing together what the child would like to do. Quality time spent with the child is another way that the soul is encouraged to stay present in the child's body and express itself. Withholding quality time can also wound. The parents might spend no quality time with the child, saying "We don't have time for you. We work hard. Time is money. You are just my child, that's all, nothing more." Children can feel very neglected if no one is really participating in their life.

On the other hand, a parent may try to control the time spent with the child. The time is spent on the parent's agenda and activities only, with the child just dragged along, not really participating, only physically engaged. For example, the child may be watching a movie or playing in the bathtub. At the parent's whim, and without asking the child if he or she is ready to stop, the parent comes and interrupts the play. No consideration or respect for the child's experience is expressed, so the child learns that his or her wishes are not important. In these situations, children can feel that they have no presence, importance, or space in the world. Sometimes these children grow up to become rescuers, a role we'll get into in a bit. It's like they think, "They are more important than me. Maybe I am in the world to serve them. Maybe my whole existence is for that." As a parent, you can prevent this from happening by giving the child a time frame for ending activities, such as "You have five more minutes, and then we'll…" do whatever activity you as a parent want the child to shift to—eating dinner, taking a nap, going out to run errands, etc. This time frame allows the child to reorient and prepare to obey you without experiencing unnecessary trauma or force.

Acts of service and education

The fourth way love is expressed is through *acts of service* to the child. A parent may act as an educator for the child, helping the child to develop skills at each stage of development: toilet training, eating properly, brushing teeth, learning how to read, and other skills. Sometimes parents spend no time at all guiding their children in this way; it is a very prevalent form of neglect. The children don't learn how to do very basic things, and this can result in very embarrassing and shaming experiences in society. Children with poor hygiene can also have serious health difficulties.

The flip side of this is that a parent may expect or demand that a child accomplish tasks, then shame them when they don't show adult-level skills or competence. The parent shows the child how to do something, and when the child tries it and doesn't do it just right the first time, the parent starts criticizing and judging the child. This hurts the child's sense of self-worth and can block further learning.

Gifts, sharing, and giving

The fifth way to express love is through *gifts, sharing, and giving.* Gifts can be an expression of love, validation, and appreciation. An example might be a special food that belongs to the parents that is given to the child or shared together, or a gift that the child wants and can use and play with as desired. But it can happen that a child has no idea what to do with a gift, and then it is not a thoughtful gift.

If children are given something that they cannot touch or play with—something they might break or get dirty—they may grow up to be adults who are unable to appreciate a gift, a vacation, or free time. They may buy many things that they cannot consume, things they can't use or don't need, which confuses real needs with imaginary desires.

Gift-giving can be neglectful or abusive if the gifts are a substitute for love. We see this more and more in the developed countries. Parents spend less and less time with their children and are less involved in their care, but they compensate by giving them huge gifts, almost as if to "buy them off" with things. Even worse, parents who ignore their children push them to eat more chocolate and empty foods to fill the hole that is left by the parents' absence. Here again, there is no recognition or validation of the child's uniqueness and essence, no attempt to discover what the child really wants and enjoys. As a result, the child may think "I don't deserve anything. I don't have a fair share in life. I'm worthless."

Young children respond to all five ways of receiving love and taking it in. But, somewhere along the way, around the age of six or seven, they begin to focus and obsess on what they are *not* getting, how love is *not* being expressed, and this builds up inside of them as a wounding. Because they tend to emphasize what they didn't get, children—and that's all of us—grow up with a particular sensitivity to a specific kind of wounding. So we come into partnership as adults, and we'll often choose a situation that reflects how we were wounded because we're trying to heal our childhood wounds through our relationship.

But funny things can happen in relationships. What was missing when you were growing up is something you are still looking for in a relationship. So you choose your partner, and sometimes you get what you are looking for, but it can happen that you don't let yourself have it because you're still focused on what you didn't get. There it is, right before your eyes, that love you wanted, but a part of you still believes that you don't have it! It is a paradox.

It can also happen that your partner is giving you a lot of love in the way he or she knows how to express it, but you may be stuck on this one form of expression that you didn't get and don't feel like you are getting. You don't even recognize what you are being given. I see this sometimes with couples who come to me for therapy. The wife may say, "My husband is never with me, he's always at work." Then you find out that, in fact, that was the situation in the family when she was growing up and that's what she is really focused on. She may have experienced one (or both) of her parents as "always working." Perhaps this woman never received love at all from the working parent as a child, or maybe that parent expressed love for her in a healthy but different way than she longed for and so the child failed to realize that she was, indeed, loved.

The tragedy of a situation like this is that people still focused on what they didn't get as children may not be open to receiving the love their partner is trying to give them, and they are not able to appreciate or feel grateful for the love that is being expressed.

So ask yourself now, of the five ways of expressing love, which one did you experience most as a wounding when you were growing up? Think about how this wounding might be playing out in your partnership. For example, do you give to your partner what you were not given? This is a clue that you may be compensating for your own wound.

Woundings may not show themselves in a big way, but when you are under stress, you may feel yourself thinking, "I never get *that*. I need *that*, and it is not there." So when you are under a lot of stress and you feel disconnected from your partner, ask yourself what you long for, what you are feeling that you are missing. Is it loving touch? Supportive words? Some quality time with your partner? Gifts of some kind? A little help? When you have an argument with your partner, note which of the five types of expression brings about forgiveness and healing for you. This is the magic bullet: a clue to what is still wounded within you that still needs healing.

We've all heard it said that, until you are able to love yourself, you cannot receive love from anyone else. Until your wounding is healed, you are likely to focus on what you needed but didn't get as a child and—especially in times of stress—may transfer your resentment and sadness about feeling unloved to your partner. Before you, as a couple, can evolve to the level of divine partnership, your woundings must be consciously recognized and healed. Working together, you can help each other develop the capacity to give and receive the love each of you needs, thus heightening your capacity for divine partnership.

It can take some time to heal woundings, but if you and your partner will work together, conscious of what's really going on when you are feeling tension in your relationship, you can give each other what you feel you did not receive from your parents. If the same area is wounded for both of you, then you just have to go through the process of getting to the pain you both feel and consciously moving through it. For example, maybe neither of you received gifts; so you can go out together and buy gifts for each other, going through the process of finding just the right, most meaningful gifts. If you wish, you can make this a regular practice.

The same can be done with forgiveness. When you are having difficulties, if you have a good sense of what your partner needs—be it hugs, kind words, or whatever—it is a lot easier to reconnect and heal. For some, roses may be just the ticket to forgiveness; for others, those same roses might drive a partner into breaking all the dirty dishes on the floor. Being tuned into what your partner really needs is important!

The Codependent Triangle

The biggest wounding that we express and receive in relationships comes from a dynamic we call the codependent triangle. In codependency, we see three positions or roles that can dynamically alternate, even within one individual: *abuser, victim,* and *rescuer.*

Formation of the codependent triangle

The codependent triangle forms in the following way. Children growing up with their parents—especially if the relationship is dysfunctional and even if one of the parents is not physically in the household—can be caught in "the line of fire" between them:

Being in the middle like this can be unbearably tense and frightening to the child, who must for survival's sake find a way to alleviate the tension. The child tries to get out of the way, to move or escape or in some way change the energy dynamics in the relationship. Although this is a very complex process, it can be simply visualized like this:

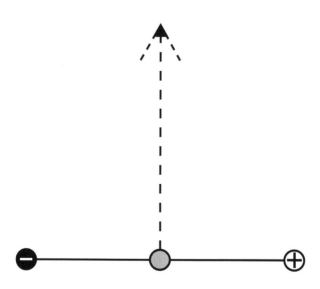

The result is a somewhat more stable relational structure, a triangle if you will. The child typically winds up in one of the three codependent roles—*abuser, victim,* or *rescuer*—with the parents in the other two positions on the triangle, as shown in the following diagram. In this way, the child achieves a certain level of predictability and balance, but at the expense of the child's soul. Parenting from a more spiritual level is crucial if a child is to avoid this unhealthy trap.

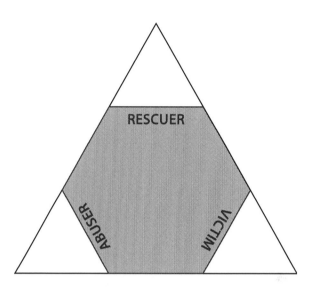

Unfortunately for many of us, the parenting we received growing up was far from spiritual, so too often we find ourselves trapped as adults in the same kind of codependent relationships we shared with our parents, incapable of spiritually parenting our own children. Without making a conscious effort to break our souls free of this prison, we are likely to wound our children in much the same ways our parents wounded us.

The good news is that wounded adults need not think of themselves as permanently "damaged goods." Our children hold an extraordinary key to our healing as adults: they can keep us connected to the spiritual side of life. When we as parents encourage and support the spiritual development of our children—their wisdom, intuition, love, creativity, and sense of wonder—we receive a clear reflection back to us of our own soul's qualities, what can be thought of as the divine inner child. We can learn ways to support our children in staying open to their authentic selves and, by doing so, heal our own past woundings as children. When we do this, we also release from our subconscious the self-limiting patterns we have internalized as children, those unhealthy energy patterns referred to as negative elementals. By encouraging children in their spiritual development, we experience the freedom to transform ourselves spiritually; by freeing them from their prison and loving them unconditionally, we free and love ourselves. But first we must become aware of which of the codependent roles and qualities we most reflect.

Codependent roles and qualities

Abuser
- active aggression
- anger
- frustration
- impatience
- violence
- arrogance
- perfectionism
- domination
- criticism of others

Maybe you say that you have never been an abuser in your life, but if you consistently express any of these qualities in your partnership or other relationships, you could well have this wound within you. Ask yourself if you respond to situations by saying (or thinking) "It's not my fault" or blaming other people for what goes wrong; these are clues that you are critical of others. Or perhaps you often say, "I know better," which can indicate you try to dominate or control other people. Although some might claim that perfectionism indicates self-control, it's really just another form of domination, of trying to control outcomes.

Victim
- helplessness
- hopelessness
- despair
- depression
- low self-esteem
- self-rejection
- shame
- fear
- isolation

You may not identify yourself as being a victim. But say somebody says to you, "You are really acting like a victim in that situation," and you say, "No, I am not a victim. I have been hurt by the other person.

That's why I feel the way I do. I feel justified to feel victimized." That is a victim position. So, too, is the act of "beating yourself up," because by being self-abusive you are making yourself out to be the victim.

Rescuer
- self-sacrifice
- suffering to love
- giving too much
- guilt
- worry
- anxiety
- the martyr syndrome
- caretaking
- enabling
- over-responsibility

Can you think of some examples of rescuing behaviors?

Codependent dynamics in families

In the codependent triangle, a kind of balancing act occurs. Let's say a child is caught between two parents playing the roles of *abuser* and *victim*. This could, for example, be an alcoholic, aggressive, frustrated father or mother; the other partner feels abused, victimized, and hurt. The child is sitting in the middle, without the skills or resources to physically escape the situation, but the situation is intolerable and must be escaped if the child is to survive. What choices may that child make? It is too stressful to be in the conflict, so the child has to take a position to feel safe. The child can either choose to side with the abuser or the victim, taking on and internalizing the unhealthy qualities of that parent, or the child must, somehow or other, alleviate the tension in the relationship.

Children want safety and order and hope that their parents will give it to them. But if the parents don't, then they have to find a position that is consistent for them. So the child must somehow balance the energy dynamics. When parents are acting out of abuser–victim roles, the abusive partner may also threaten the child if the child doesn't take that parent's side. Or the victimized partner may manipulate the child into being a victim, too. One possibility is that the child can side with one parent over the other in an effort to alleviate the tension and restore order. A second possibility is that the child cannot decide which parent to side with and so winds up caught between them. What can the child do then? Become a rescuer.

Look at the qualities of a rescuer again. Children playing the role of rescuer are not like confident adult heroes riding in on a shining steed; they painfully sacrifice themselves in a frantic effort to balance the family. The parents, as abuser and victim, really only mirror each other; like needy children, neither one feels truly powerful or in charge, and both feel unloved and unacknowledged by their partner. They both want the same thing, but they go about getting it in different ways. So the child might say, "There is no king or queen at home, so I have to be in charge." Taking on too much responsibility is another quality of the rescuer.

Children who take on the role of queen or king can grow up very fast. They don't really have a childhood. A lot of first-born or only children take this position. First-born and only children have very similar dynamics. The difference is that only children take on the roles of both the first-born and the last-born child: very responsible, very mature on one side, and very flimsy and immature on the other side. If there is more than one child in a family, then the roles may get distributed. Perhaps the first-born child becomes the rescuer and the second-born child becomes a victim. The middle child usually witnesses everything that is going on in the family system. Of course, every family is different, and the relationships can be very complex.

Let's look at some other possible codependent dynamics. The child may be thrust between one parent who is a caretaker or rescuer and the other who is really a victim. The classic example of this family dynamic is after a war, when the men come home totally traumatized and wounded and the women play the role of major caretaker. The woman might be caretaking the spouse, who takes on the roles of both victim and aggressor. Another example is when one parent is really ill, mentally or physically ill, and the abuser or victim spouse is thrust into the caretaking role. In these mixed cases, the child can still be caught up in tension between the two.

What can happen to a child in such a position? It can happen that the child acts out aggressively. In another situation, the rescuer might spend too much time with the other partner while the child is neglected. Then the child may think "I will get attention if I become a victim, too" or "The only way that I am going to get any attention is if I join the rescuer and take care of the victim." Either way, the child is forced to take a position to balance the relationship.

If one parent is functioning as the rescuer and the other is the abuser, normally the caretaker is trying to take care of the child, to protect the child from abuse. A classic situation of this type is the molestation and physical abuse of the child. The caretaker tries to protect the child from the abuser. What would the child do in that situation? The child is most likely to be a victim. In families where both parents are caught up in abusive behaviors toward their children, the victims must also come to their own rescue.

Whenever a child feels too much stress in a codependent situation and cannot find a way out, then that child will become ill or even die, which is the only way to escape the system. Usually this happens when a child is between an abuser and a victim. Maybe someone else in the family, a sibling perhaps, already has the rescuer role, so the child can't adopt that strategy to ease the tension. Physical illness is a common way out, because if the child takes the position of victim, the victim–parent's role has to shift to rescuer to keep the family dynamics in balance. Children are clever enough to survive. If one parent is missing through death or divorce, a child might take on the role of the missing parent, at least energetically.

As you can see, relationships where there is wounding in the family can be very, very complicated, but the dynamics are easy to understand when you reduce them to this codependent triangle. As long as you are bound up in the triangle, you are a prisoner; your soul is in prison. You grow up, leave home, and go out to live your life, and maybe you forget what happened—at least on the surface—but the training in relationships that you received as a child is still sitting in your subconscious. Then when you form a partnership with a significant other, what role do you take on? The role you learned to play in childhood, or perhaps an opposing one. Or you might try shifting roles, unconsciously trying out different positions in different partner-ships to see what feels the most comfortable and safe for you. If you are a rescuer, you will identify with the rescuer role and probably attract a victim or an abuser as your partner. If you attract an abuser, it could be because of an unconscious need to have children to protect against an aggressor so you can play the role of a rescuer again. Or you may choose a victim to continue caretaking. Or you may have an aggressive child.

So think to yourself now: *When I was young, what was my primary role in my family, and what did I have to change about myself to take that position?*

To tie this back in to the male–female energies we covered earlier, *abuser* is an unhealthy male energy and *victim* is an unhealthy female energy; *rescuer* energy can come from either polarity. Some rescuers are very male-polarized with very active, *yang* energy because that is what is needed to get things done: accomplish tasks, offer protection, make the money. Or maybe what is needed is nurturing and love. Maybe a mother with several young children gets ill and the oldest daughter thinks she has to be the mother and step in to soothe and reassure her younger siblings. Then the rescuing is expressed more from the feminine side and more feminine qualities are apparent. In some cases, people will express unhealthy male and female qualities at the same time, but this is rare. So, whatever choice you made as a child, now you may polarize yourself to one side or the other and neglect the opposite aspect within yourself.

For instance, say you are a little girl. One of your parents is very weak and the other is stronger but not in charge. To be a good rescuer, you have to become totally male-polarized, so you take charge and you do everything to make it work. Or you can go the other way, totally into your female energy, especially if you have a totally victimized mother who says "Can you give me a hug?" You then might become this kind of hugging rescuer.

It can also happen that a girl whose father has a healthy female energy but a wounded male energy will get nurturing from her father as if he were the mother, but also develop more of her male traits. Then, when she grows up, she may seek out relationships where she can express more male energy while also seeking a mother in the man.

These are only a few examples of how these energy dynamics can play out in relationships. If you polarize toward one side or the other, you lose your balance and become trapped. This is what happens to most children coming from dysfunctional families until they learn, usually as adults, how to balance these energies in healthy ways. Until they are able to do this, however, their souls remain imprisoned.

Some children manage to find a way out of the prison of the soul. The way is contained in the impulse that initially propelled them into the prison to begin with: to lift themselves out of an intolerable position. Unfortunately, some children exit the codependent triangle through fatal accidents, by becoming emotionally dysfunctional, or by dying emotionally to themselves. Luckily, there is another way, a spiritual way. Actually, spirituality is the only way out of the prison of the soul.

Children who die early or almost die, for example, actually want to take the spiritual position; some part of them knows that this is the way out. They want to test and see if their parents really want them or if anyone else will come along and show them that love exists in this world. If somebody then steps forward to express love in a healthy way, then the child actually has another position to take, and a more compassionate and spiritual perspective of the situation. Perhaps there is an aunt, an uncle, a teacher, a neighbor, or a caretaker who is able to give the child a healthier point of reference—someone who serves as a guiding light, who makes an enormous impression of love on the child. Or perhaps a guardian angel takes the child into the light; the child has a near-death experience and comes back with another viewpoint.

If love replaces neglect and dysfunction as their primary reality, some children are able to survive living with dysfunctional parents until it's possible for them to move out. This doesn't mean life is easy, but such children can see the situation from a more spiritual perspective and so are no longer in prison. Unfortunately for some children, if no love comes forth and they cannot find a spiritual way out of their prison, they may surrender and say, "I come." And so they leave, and then they may hover about the family system like a little angel for a while, and in that position may witness and understand what they could not understand while they were alive. Some children may simply remove themselves from the situation by escaping into fantasy, which is how they are able to go somewhere else without physically dying.

So, whatever position you took as a child, when you grow up and get into a partnership, you can recreate the situation that you are familiar with from your family system. This is how subconscious elementals work, actually, by attracting a similar situation or partnership, even if you do not consciously want it to happen that way.

It can also happen that you play out all three codependent roles within your family, at your workplace, and in your friendships. A man came to me for therapy. At work he was the boss, and people were terrified by him. When he was at home, his wife was the boss, and he was the victim. His children were caught up in this dynamic, so when he was with his children, he became their rescuer. This man thus took all three roles, but in different areas in his life. This is quite common.

If you find yourself playing all three roles, ask yourself which one you mostly adopt. What is your main role at home with your family, when you are at work, or in other situations? Does your role change in these different settings? If so, or if not, what might this suggest?

Something else that can happen is that a person gets disenchanted or bored with playing one role and will then flip into another. For example, a rescuer taking care of a victim gets burned out and has no more energy to expend in rescuing. Say it's a mother rescuing a child completely neglected by the father. The father quits at the end of his work day, withdrawing into the television with a beer and his remote, ignoring his wife and child. As far as he's concerned, he's done his work for the day. The wife keeps cleaning up the kitchen while trying in vain to get the kid to do homework, and she's planning the next day's meals and getting their school and work clothes ready for the next day. She's tired, and she gets more and more angry that nobody else is making any kind of effort. So she blows up and yells, "I'm out of here! I'm leaving!" But not before she flips into the role of abuser and starts giving everybody some hell.

When a parent switches from being a rescuer to an abuser, the victim is completely shocked. The one person who was paying attention to and caring for the victim is now screaming, threatening to leave, and perhaps being violent. Clearly, this is very confusing and very hurtful for a child victim. There are a number of ways these abrupt changes in role can happen in families, and long-lasting wounds can be formed.

When you think about it, given how complex our relationships are and how many factors are involved, it is a miracle that people can even talk to each other. This is probably why many societies in the world have such strong, rigid expectations about how men, women, and male and female children should behave because, otherwise, things might really get out of hand. The answer, however, is not to control people—who, as we have discussed, embody both *yin* and *yang* energies—by forcing them into rigid female or male roles. The answer is to transform the codependent triangle into a kind of divine trinity by elevating *abuser, victim,* and *rescuer* to their respective spiritual counterparts. This is how we can escape the soul's prison and move toward the highest expression of love—divine love—for ourselves and in partnership. This truly divine alchemical process will be our focus for the rest of this book.

In the work to follow, and in the meditations, you will always begin by centering yourself in stillness—especially if you find yourself becoming confused. These teachings are not linear, and grasping them involves more than just a conscious understanding of the concepts. It will help to allow your focus to be a little bit fuzzy, holistic, and right-brained. Centering yourself in stillness helps you achieve this state.

Centering can be accomplished in a number of ways, so just choose whatever way works best for you. You may already have a technique you use to center yourself, or you can try one of the following ways of reaching a place of awake, inner stillness.

- Close your eyes, breathe deeply, and visualize yourself in a column of white or golden light. Fill yourself with this light.
- Breathe deeply, focus on your heart, and repeat to yourself several times a sacred name for the divine, such as "Love," "God," or "Hu."
- With your attention on your breath, breathe consciously and deeply three to five times.

Meditation to center in stillness

Take a moment to step back from your outer awareness, emptying yourself of concerns or any need to think about anything, and just be in a place of inner stillness.

From Codependency to Divine Union in Partnership

SO, HOW CAN the codependent triangle, with all its dense, dysfunctional energetic solidity, be transformed into a divine trinity? And what does that even mean? In the doctrine of the trinity in Christianity, the divine is depicted as "God in three persons": Father, Son, and Holy Spirit. These three aspects are indivisibly bound together in one being referred to as God. Similarly, Hinduism holds that all creation is sustained by a partnership of three great gods working together as one: Brahma, the creator, Vishnu, the preserver, and Shiva, the destroyer. Similar concepts of divine union are prevalent in religious, psychological, and political thought. For example: "United we stand, divided we fall"; *E pluribus unum*, out of many, one.

In the codependent triangle, *abuser, victim,* and *rescuer* are also bound together as one inseparable energetic system. As we've seen already, this accounts in part for its rigidity. The energies of all the players in the relationship are bound up in maintaining the system, subconsciously if not consciously, no matter how dysfunctional it becomes over time. In other words, the codependent triangle may look like a trinity, but it is hardly divine.

What must happen is that the energies bound up in the codependent triangle must be redirected and the system opened up so that the healthy, more spiritual energies of divine love pervade the system. This is a multidimensional, divine alchemical process that is difficult to convey in a linear fashion. You can think of it in terms of shifting your focus from being on the inside of your prison to extending through and beyond its walls. Inside the prison, each person in the relationship is confined to a lonely cell; all they can seem to do is beat the bars of their cage. When partners help each other step out of their codependent roles—unlock the doors, escape from the prison, and come together in the light of the spiritual realm—they unite to set everyone free. From this state of being, divine love is expressed and the codependent triangle simply collapses. This is what is meant by divine union in partnership.

The following diagram is a simplified framework to help you visualize how this occurs. The outer triangle represents the spiritual realm that transcends the individual. Note how *abuser, victim,* and *rescuer* now face out of their soul's prison, each in the direction of a more unified, spiritual position.

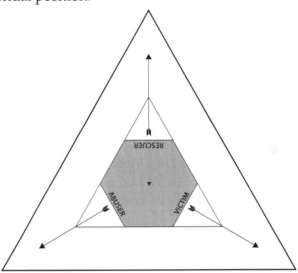

The Four-stage Path to Divine Union

The codependent triangle is energetically dense and solid, and collapsing it involves each partner pursuing a four-stage path customized to his or her predominant codependent role. Fundamentally (as we'll discuss in considerable depth in the next section, *Evolution of Divine Love in Partnership*), this is an energetic process. Each partner's path, while different in the particulars, involves working through the same three levels—physical, emotional, and mental—to reach the fourth, the ultimate, spiritual level, thereby escaping and transcending the soul's prison.

Whenever you see a pyramid-path icon in the materials that follow, know that it conveys all four stages of the path as well as its culmination in divine union.

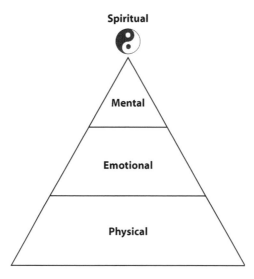

As the above diagram suggests, the spiritual level, the fourth stage of the path, lies beyond the confines of the individual; it is a state of energetic balance and wholeness as implied by the *yin–yang* symbol at the apex of the pyramid. Spiritual transformation is initiated by identifying the role (or roles) that you play in your codependent relationship. Once this is done, each partner then follows the four-stage path customized for his or her role, which ultimately results in the evolved and balanced energies and aspects of the divine trinity—divine union, and divine love, in partnership:

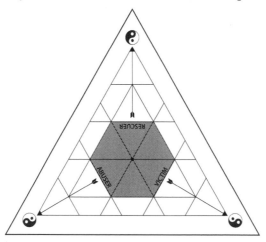

As partners, you can help each other identify the codependent roles that you play with each other and transform them into their divine counterparts. As unhealthy energies, or negative elementals, are transformed into more healthy ones, the two of you begin to activate the three-fold energy of the divine trinity. Ultimately, you transcend codependency, uniting in spirit, empowered to give and receive divine love. In the light of this love, the energetic density of the codependent triangle cannot be sustained. Even if a third person, such as a child, is playing a role in the triangle but is not involved with the transformative work, he or she will adjust to the changing energy dynamics to keep the system in balance, as always. This time, however, the balance that is achieved is spiritually healthy.

Now, as we discussed before, people can take on different roles depending on the particular situation they are in—at work, at home, and so forth. As you work through this material, stay focused on which role you are *most* invested in with your partner. As you become more skilled in the spiritual transformation process, you will be able to apply what you learn together to other situations where your roles may be very different. So, ask yourself now, *What is my predominant codependent role in my relationship with my partner?* This is the path you will follow in the work to come. Your partner's role and path will be different from, but complementary to, yours.

On the following pages, the main qualities of the *abuser, victim,* and *rescuer* roles that we have already covered are broken down into the physical, emotional, and mental stages of the path. You can think of the spiritual states listed for each respective role as goals or outcomes you are aiming for as you work on transformation.

Take some time, working with your partner, to decide which paths to follow before going forward. Examine the iconic representation of your own path and commit it to memory. From this point on, we will draw more heavily on visualizations like these to convey complex material in a way that will be easier for you to understand and integrate.[3]

The exercises at the end of this book refer to the *abuser, victim,* and *rescuer* paths. It will be helpful, before doing an exercise, to refer back to the graphics on the following pages to help you stay focused on what you are trying to accomplish.

---

[3] *You may also want to ponder how the material we have covered up through this section might fit in with the master diagram on the back cover—but only if you feel ready to do so.*

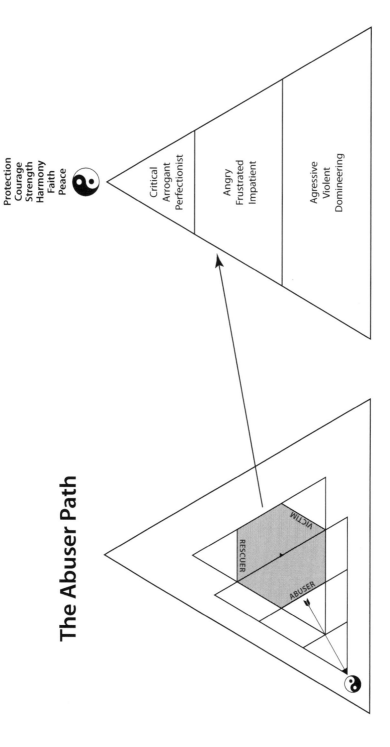

The Abuser Path

Protection
Courage
Strength
Harmony
Faith
Peace

Critical
Arrogant
Perfectionist

Angry
Frustrated
Impatient

Agressive
Violent
Domineering

VICTIM

RESCUER

ABUSER

ABUSER QUALITIES AND SPIRITUAL TRANSFORMATION

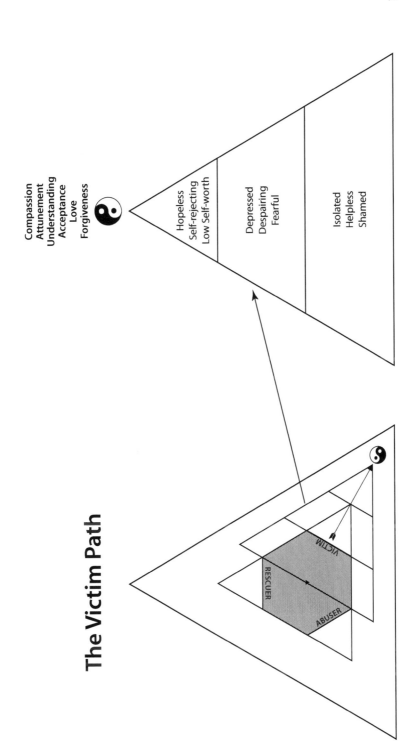

The Victim Path

Compassion
Attunement
Understanding
Acceptance
Love
Forgiveness

Hopeless
Self-rejecting
Low Self-worth

Depressed
Despairing
Fearful

Isolated
Helpless
Shamed

RESCUER

VICTIM

ABUSER

VICTIM QUALITIES AND SPIRITUAL TRANSFORMATION

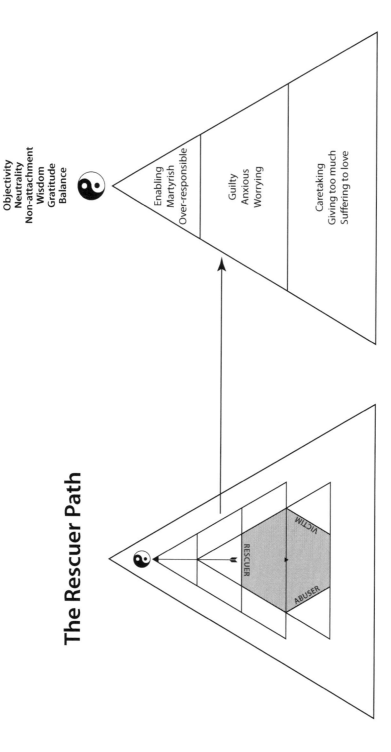

The Rescuer Path

Objectivity
Neutrality
Non-attachment
Wisdom
Gratitude
Balance

Enabling
Martyrish
Over-responsible

Guilty
Anxious
Worrying

Caretaking
Giving too much
Suffering to love

VICTIM

RESCUER

ABUSER

RESCUER QUALITIES AND SPIRITUAL TRANSFORMATION

Evolution of Divine Love in Partnership

YOU CAN SAY that in our society we don't put the right emphasis on what relationships are really about. Many people think of the relationship between two loving partners in terms of physical embrace and romance, which is not even half of it, and don't recognize the potential for the deeper, more enduring dynamics of divine love. Relationships go through four distinct stages as they evolve toward this higher level of expression, and if you are focused on just the beginning stages, you may mistakenly believe your relationship is not doing well, stay trapped in codependent struggles, and miss out on the joys that divine partnership can bring.

We will now look at the four stages of relationship, which you can think of as steps on the four-stage path to divine love. To begin, I want to share some examples from history and literature, stories that teach us about divine love. Keep in the back of your mind the pyramid-path you chose in the last chapter, because it will have personal meaning for you as we go through these stories.

Teaching Stories of Divine Love

The Story of Psyche and Eros

The first teaching story is a very famous one, first written down in the second century by the Roman author Apuleius: the story of Psyche and Eros. This myth shows how the process of divine union takes place in stages. Most of the stories about the gods are about their attraction to mortals; the mythic literature is full of tales of one-night encounters that hardly involved commitments or marriage. For example, the god Zeus had a wife named Hera, but he also had a lot of concubines and a lot of children out of wedlock. Such stories are mostly focused on the first level of relationship, physical desire. An exception is the story of Psyche and Eros, which shows the transformation of a relationship, a movement through the different stages.

Psyche was a beautiful young woman, vivacious and popular, and she was becoming a rival of Aphrodite, the goddess of love. Psyche represents youthful beauty. Aphrodite became rather jealous of Psyche because no one was honoring the goddess, they were just worshipping Psyche's beauty. So Aphrodite decided to get rid of her. She tied Psyche up on top of a mountain, determined to leave her there until she died.

While Psyche was on the mountain, the son of Aphrodite—Eros, the god of love—happened to be flying by. When he saw Psyche, he was delighted by her and came down and asked, "What are you doing here?" At that moment, he was swept away by this incredible desire for her. So he took her away and hid her in some honeymoon place, and they were very happy. But Eros had one requirement for Psyche: that she was never allowed to see who he really was. This symbolizes the first stage of relationship, the "voice of me," and Eros wanted to keep it at that level.

Now, Psyche was not content to stay at this first stage. She was drawn to the second stage, the "voice of us." She wanted to know who it was she loved, and she wanted them to be together in the light of day as well as in the dark of night. So one night when Eros was asleep, Psyche held a lamp up to his face and was shocked to see that he was not mortal, that he was a youthful god. When Eros woke up and caught Psyche looking at him, he left her, and Psyche was left with a deep longing that only her beloved Eros could fulfill. The German poet, Goethe, called this "the holy longing" or longing for the divine. It is the desire for something invisible, something beyond one's self, a longing to be swept into a higher feeling of love.

Psyche wanted Eros very much, and she wanted to get him back somehow, so she went to Aphrodite for help. When Aphrodite saw Psyche, she thought to herself, "I couldn't kill her, so I will get rid of her in another way. But if she passes my tests, she will be worthy of the love of my son." Aphrodite gave Psyche many labors to perform. She also tried to discipline her son Eros, to teach him that leaving Psyche wasn't the proper thing to do and that he needed to show more respect for the mortals and for himself.

After that Psyche and Eros had each worked at it for a while, Zeus told Aphrodite that "this precious, courageous young woman, Psyche, is worthy to be your daughter-in-law." So Psyche and Eros got married, reaching a level of commitment to each other, and they had a child together named Pleasure. To the ancient Greeks, "pleasure" meant bliss or divine union. So we can see that Psyche and Eros went through different stages in their relationship, evolving toward divine union and ultimately finding harmony and peace together. But it wasn't easy; they had to go through trials.

The idea of divine union in literature, operas, and mythology always involves trials or challenges. You see this same theme very clearly expressed in Mozart's opera, *The Magic Flute*. The hero and heroine fall in love, but they have to earn the right to divine union and true marriage. The lovers are separated for long periods of time, longing for each other, and they have to learn to surrender their human desire for something greater. Finally, they triumph through their surrender. It is interesting that the sound of the flute in *The Magic Flute* has a very spiritual sound—the sound of the soul—and this sound guided them to their final union.

The Story of Baucis and Philemon

Another story of true devotion involves the third stage of development in relationships, the "voice of the world." One day the gods Zeus and Hermes were a little bored and said to themselves, "Humanity has gone to hell, and nobody down there has real generosity. If we can find just one generous person or couple that is living truthfully, we will give them our kingdom." So they went down to Earth disguised as wanderers and started going from home to home asking for food, water, and shelter. Many people shut their door, sending the gods away, and some even threw things at them. None of them realized that they were rejecting the gods.

Finally the gods come to a very humble place, the home of a couple named Baucis and Philemon. When they knocked on the door, the couple opened it and welcomed the strangers into their home. The gods noticed that the house was harmonious and the man and woman were in love with each other. The couple began to prepare a meal for them. Wine was served in wooden cups that Baucis had carved himself. The meal was gathered from the garden, the milk from their own goats, the honey from their bees, and the fruit from their own trees. There was a wonderful warmth and light in the couple's presence, and Zeus and Hermes were very moved by this. "This is true love," they thought to themselves.

Suddenly, after the wine was gone, the cups began to fill up again automatically. Zeus and Hermes revealed themselves to Baucis and Philemon and said: "We are going to punish your neighbors because they would not show any generosity towards us. They were engaged in only selfish desires. They never welcomed us." Zeus said to the couple, "I will give you anything you want. If you want a castle, I will give you a castle, or youthfulness, beauty, whatever you desire." But Baucis and Philemon said to the gods, "What we would like to be are your priests and to guard your temples. And because we have spent many happy years together and can't live without each other, we would like to die together." This represents the third stage of relationship, with the qualities of devotion and commitment.

The couple's prayer was granted by Zeus. Baucis and Philemon lived on for a long time together. One day, while talking over the old days spent together, they watched each other begin to turn into trees. Baucis became a linden tree and Philemon became an oak, and they continued to grow side by side, joined at the trunk, their branches intertwining as one. This story demonstrates a purity of love that moves the gods by its beauty and harmony, a love that results in a beautiful feeling of unity.

Other expressions of unity are abundant. One is found in stories about the union of the mystic and the beloved. For example, in the Christian church a nun is considered to be the bride of Christ. This relationship is a spiritual marriage, a divine union where humility, intimacy, and love are the dominant characteristics. The nun has a deeply committed personal relationship and divine partnership with God through spiritual dialogue and prayer. Saint Theresa of Avila, who exemplified this divine level of relationship and called it "this fever of God," maintained that the union was mysterious and a great delight; that, as far as can be understood, the soul is made one with the spirit of God, who is pleased to show us his love. We see the same expression of unity in alchemy. Many alchemical symbols convey the story of Adam and Eve. When Adam and Eve left the Garden of Eden, they experienced separation not only from God but from each other. The only way they could reconcile this separation was to come together again in androgyny, which means having both male and female qualities within oneself. The cross is another very powerful symbol. In religious teachings, the cross represents the crucifixion, but there is a lot more to it than that. The cross shows divine union of earth and heaven, male and female, with the center being the point of union. The cross also represents the union of the four elements: earth, fire, water and air. This is the divine alchemy.

The Story of Hercules

Hercules had a big temper. He was polarized in unhealthy male energy. He had a music teacher, and one day he got frustrated because Hercules couldn't play his instrument correctly. In his anger, Hercules just killed the music teacher. The gods wanted to teach Hercules some lessons, so Hermes gave Hercules some work to do on androgyny. He sold Hercules to a mortal queen named Omphale. In Greek, *omphalos* means the navel, the chi center. What Hercules had to do to balance his male and female energies was to dress as a woman during the day, cook for the queen, and do all the household things a housewife would do for her husband. At night, Hercules had to be the man and make love with the queen. This was Hercules' yoga practice, and by doing it every day, he was able to achieve androgyny. He put himself in the shoes of the other side and learned that both male and female energies are valid. Hercules had become too polarized toward the male side and unhealthy male aggressiveness when he killed his music teacher. To find balance, he had to learn about the female side. Eventually Hercules did learn and was released.

The Story of Naroda

Another story of androgyny is about a very old Indian philosopher named Naroda. Naroda was very, very arrogant. He would have nothing to do with women or female energy. He thought women were not even made by God, that they had no spirit and were like animals. So one day the god Vishnu and goddess Laksmi were in a tantric reunion. Naroda was just walking by the forest at the time, and when he saw the gods he judged their action to be ungodly. In order to teach Naroda a lesson, Vishnu put Naroda into a sacred pool of water. Water and baptisms were a symbol of androgyny to the ancients. Vishnu dipped Naroda into the water and turned him into a woman. So Naroda, the woman, then had to get married. She had to perform all the duties of a wife, and she had three children, all of them boys. Naroda gave the boys all the love a mother would give to her children. When the boys grew up, Naroda had to experience all three boys going off to war and being killed, and she had to suffer the deep sorrow of a mother witnessing her children die. Only at that point was Naroda changed back into male form.

The idea of water and androgyny was very common with the ancients. In ancient Greece, a special ritual was used for initiates of the priesthood. These young men and women were trained to jump off a cliff and dive into the ocean. Their initiation into the mystery of androgyny was that they had to fast for a long period of time, and then they had to take special herbs and dive into the water. Fifty percent achieved androgyny and survived; the other fifty percent achieved androgyny and did not survive. So, either way, the initiates met their goal! They experienced the ego's death and the oceanic feeling of being one with the cosmos. This ritual has endured to this day on certain islands in Greece in the form of young men going sponge diving in the spring.

Jesus' baptism by John the Baptist is another example of plunging into the waters of androgyny, of divine alchemy, and reemerging transformed. Ceremonially putting water on the forehead is another example. This was a Gnostic ritual of recreating the communion between Jesus and Mary Magdalene. You can find examples of androgyny throughout religion, such as in the relationships between male and female saints. Saint Frances and Saint Claire expressed great respect for divine reunion and holy love. Saint Theresa and Saint John of the Cross are another example of deep spiritual bonds and a feeling of divine love.

Four Stages in the Evolution of Divine Love

As we touched on before, divine love evolves through four stages. This evolutionary process is reflected in our relationships and in the movement of energy through the chakras of our own bodies. Look at the following triangle:

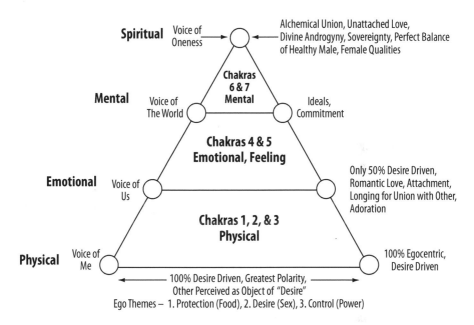

Note that the four stages are not exclusive; you can be working on more than one at the same time. I'll give you some brief meditations that you can do at home to help you move more fluidly through the stages.

Stage 1: Physical, "Voice of Me"

The first stage in relationship is what we call physical attraction. At this stage, desire is the strongest for an object. In a relationship, this would be where two people see each other as providing protection, food, sex, power—basic instinctual things and needs. At this level of relationship, the partner is seen as more of an object than a person. The lust energy that connects to the other is dominant: "I desire you. I want you. I expect you to give me this and that," etc. This type of relationship basically involves the first three chakras. It is the most dualistic state. It may look like a marriage or partnership, but in fact it's survival-oriented. Some of you may have grown up in a family where this was the main theme between your mother and father. This is the first stage of relationship and, in the case of some couples, this is as far as they go.

Why wouldn't a marital relationship develop past the first stage? Some couples are not able to evolve because they don't have good role models, or their hearts were so wounded as children that they stay at the first stage as a way of avoiding intimacy. The first stage is safe. Nothing else has to get done. No pain has to be faced, and no effort has to be made beyond the basic survival level. Unfortunately, a lot of relationships are still stuck in this survival-level energy. This kind of relationship and connectedness to a partner is based on what I call the "voice of me": *my* needs. I have seen couples who came to me because they were having a lot of trouble with each other. They would say to each other, "You don't give me this or that." This is very ego-based consciousness. It is narcissistic. But, at this stage, divine love is beginning to express a very basic connectedness between male and female. It is a beginning.

Meditation: Each evening before bedtime, review any negative or problematic behaviors, thoughts, or feelings you had during the day. Examine these events carefully, and then say to yourself, "What I was thinking or feeling today of a negative nature that I should not have been thinking or feeling was …. What I could have thought or felt in a better way was…." Then reframe the event or situation in your imagination, returning to the situation but seeing it with a positive outcome. Do this same process for any negative behaviors. This exercise builds positive elementals of change.

Stage 2: Emotional, "Voice of Us"

The next stage of divine love is the emotional stage, and it involves the fourth and fifth chakras. At this second stage of relationship, our desire for the other is elevated to a more astral level. I call this stage the "voice of us." It is a state of being together. Here, the feeling is not so much that of lust or desire but that of longing, of wanting to be with the other, of wanting to get lost in the other. This is romantic longing. It is a feeling of missing something, of being incomplete, and seeking union with another to make yourself complete. In a partnership situation, this normally results in emotional bonding. The two people become concerned for each other. There is the real desire to get to know the other, to care for and honor the other. Quite often at this level of relationship, the couple will form a partnership through marriage. At this stage of relationship, you communicate with each other, and you take the time to understand your partner's position. There are no objects anymore; there are real human beings who have feelings. You express care and love.

While the first stage is *egocentric,* this second stage is more focused on family as the source of love—but not so much the world or external surroundings. At this stage, the couple may be somewhat invested in the immediate community where they live, but normally not with the world at large or the "bigger picture" of things. We call this being *ethnocentric.* At this level, one can have balance in relation to the family situation, but typically the values of this consciousness don't extend very much beyond the family. Everything is in order in the family, but we don't care about how the neighbors are doing. This is a kind of "clan" way of thinking. At the first stage, the other person is not very important and you don't really know them. On the second level you begin to see the other and can begin to appreciate the other's point of view.

Meditation: Visualize white light flowing up your feet and into your whole body. When you are filled with this light, see yourself walking into a beautiful garden. Bring your partner or another person you are having problems with into the garden and share your uncensored sentiments with them. Now, imagine yourself stepping out of your physical body, your mind and heart, and attuning yourself to the other person's body, mind, and heart on a deeper level of love and desire to understand their experience. Then return to yourself. What insight and awareness do you now have to share?

Stage 3: Mental, "Voice of the World"

At the third stage, the level of commitment and devotion, you move to the sixth and seventh chakras. The polarity is much less intense here on the mental level. You are moving toward union, coming closer and closer to each other. We call this the "voice of all of us" or the "voice of the world." At this stage, you can be of service to your ideals together, and maybe you are working together for a higher good or purpose. There is a kind of unity in your focus on helping and serving the world together. Because you have your relationship, you already have connectedness, so this is no longer the central issue as it was at the second stage. From this sense of connectedness, you can help others outside of your relationship.

At this stage, the energy of desire or lust for the other is much less. There is more spiritual discipline and obedience to the divine ideal. You are doing everything in the name of Christ, God, Spirit. You are in a process of surrender, more and more letting go of whatever keeps you divided from yourself and the beloved within you. You are totally obedient to the divine within you. Or, in the case of your relationship with another person, this is the place of acceptance. There is much more of a feeling of working as a team. At this stage of relationship, the issue is not so much with each other as partners, but of how do we stand together in the world, what do we do, how do we serve, how do we grow in a higher way. At this point, the focus may be more about spirituality, how can you support each other in your inner evolution.

In mystical literature you see the devotional level expressed quite often. Here are some examples of this third stage. The disciple is going around crying and lost and wanting to just wash the feet of the teacher. Nothing else is important in life. This can go on for years and can be very dramatic. When the guru of one of my teachers died physically, this man was so devoted to him that he cried so long and so hard that he actually became blind in one eye. He was in constant agony over the loss. The romantic stage is also reflected by the troubadours of the Renaissance. Singing songs to the beloved became almost like a high art form. This process of romantic love is an evolution of the dynamic between male and female. Then at the devotional level, one becomes a complete servant with the divine. This is a kind of duty in the face of every difficulty. Saint Frances said "God brings me the sunshine and God brings me the rain, but it doesn't matter. I am grateful for everything."

Somewhere between the second and third stage, a time comes that we call "the dark night of the soul." This is when you feel like God has gone away, that you have been abandoned. The mystics called this feeling desolation. What is really happening is that the ego—for it is the ego that maintains a sense of separation—is in the process of dying so that you can realize who you really are and come fully into yourself.

Meditation: Repeat the garden meditation you did for the emotional level, except this time call the Christ self, or spiritual guide of your choosing, into the garden. After attuning to your partner as before and sharing new insights, step into the spiritual self and hear his words: "My healing hands are your healing hands, my light your light, my heart of love your heart of love. Step into my light, love, healing hands, my body and my blood—I am your energetic vitality." Now, view the original situation from this third position of neutrality, wisdom, power and love.

Stage 4: Spiritual, "Voice of Oneness"

As you and your partner progress through the stages, more and more your relationship begins to reflect your spirituality in such a way that, sooner or later, you reach the fourth stage, divine union. This union happens not between the partners but within each individual in the relationship. You are both autonomous and independent beings, you respect and love each other, and you honor the values you share. At this stage of relationship, you may be very different people in many ways, but you unify yourselves. On the highest level, this means that you each express healthy male and female qualities, what Carl Jung referred to as divine androgyny. Even without a partner, this process is taking place; as long as you have a relationship with something, like relationship with God, you will go through the four stages of divine love. Some mystics choose a solitary path of life, and they still go through these stages.

So the fourth stage, divine union, is spiritual love. This is unconditional love. This is accepting your partner for who they are and allowing them to be themselves. It is fully honoring your partner and yourself. Spiritual love represents an ability to love the other person as you love yourself.

This fourth, and highest, stage is not easy to achieve because the ego likes to fight forever. It creates fight and flight reactions. In the first three stages, there tends to be a lot of struggle because the ego is trying to get what it wants or what it thinks it wants. There are many expectations and disappointments, and this disappointment leads to suffering because the ego doesn't get what it thinks it should have gotten. But in divine union, there is nothing to fight; there is only the wish to love more and more. When you fall in love with the mystery of love, it lifts and carries you.

In essence, as you move through the four stages, you are moving from a greater sense of duality to oneness. In this process, with whomever you have committed to living your life with, you gradually withdraw your projections and expectations of your partner. Personal suffering becomes love and peace, and the freedom to love increases progressively.

Meditation: Lift into a column of light and rise up into the garden of your soul. In the garden are the energies of your divine, archetypal mother and father, the perfect male–female energies of Mother God and Father God. Attune to them and feel their healthy male and female qualities as your qualities. Feel your oneness with them as they hold you in their arms, in the warm embrace of divine love. Feel your sovereignty, independence, love, and freedom. Look at your life and relationships from this perspective and viewpoint. Return slowly from your soul's garden, and then back to your physical awareness.

Learning Androgyny

SO, UP TO THIS point, you have learned about healthy male and female qualities, which are sometimes referred to as virtues, and you have a better sense of why you and your partner might express unhealthy qualities and have difficulties in your relationship. You understand how you can become trapped together in a prison of codependency, and you have seen that love for your partner can evolve far beyond the physical and romantic stages of relationship to its highest level of expression in divine androgyny. In divine androgyny, you realize that you and the other person are one, that your soul and their soul are ultimately the same. So, what keeps you from reaching this state of being androgynous? Let's turn our attention now to elementals.

Elementals: The Voices of Conflict

Basically, there are two types of elementals: negative and positive. In psychology, negative elementals are referred to as "fixed desire thoughts," which are enduring emotion–thought complexes. With negative elementals, desires or feelings precede and color our thoughts and subsequent actions in a negative way, such as when we become volatile when we are angry. Positive elementals, on the other hand, are called "thought desires." These are enduring thought–emotion complexes, with thought preceding emotion and grounding us energetically. For now, we are primarily concerned with the negative ones and how they are created.

Creation of elementals

An elemental is created from etheric energy. We humans create elementals all the time. In the case of negative elementals, this is how it begins: Say you have a strong desire for something. You want to fill some kind of emptiness within yourself, to fulfill some need that you feel is not fulfilled. So you go out looking for an object to satisfy your desire, like the Prodigal Son wasting his energy on fast living, trying to get satisfaction from the outside world. With a negative elemental, when you reach out and fulfill your desire through obtaining this object, there may be a temporary feeling of satisfaction or peace, but then the desire quickly returns and you repeat the same process with another object—and then another. This feeds the negative elemental, and its energy grows. Every time you give in to the desire to fulfill the need, the elemental grows within your consciousness until it begins to enslave you. This is what psychologists call addiction, and it can lead to being powerless to stop doing whatever it is you are doing—eating, drinking, gambling, or any number of behaviors that people become addicted to. When you find yourself in this situation, the negative elemental has taken control of you.

When we create elementals, not only are they located in the physical brain matter, but they also become like entities living in our minds and energy fields. Elementals are energetic phenomena. They contain information and a little program that you have written for them. Perhaps the program is: "I want chocolates," and maybe now your chocolate elemental says, "There is nothing wrong with chocolate!" That chocolate elemental is a cute little elemental, isn't it? So say you begin to feel a cute little desire for chocolates, but it starts getting pretty strong. One day at work, you try a good chocolate that somebody has brought in. You linger over its taste with pleasure and say, "I would like to have this again. And again. And again." One day your colleague brings in a box of the same type of chocolate and puts it into the refrigerator. At first your elemental is somewhat civilized. It waits until your colleague offers you one. But then, after some time, this elemental says, "You know, I can go and just sneak a little bit out of the refrigerator. No one will know." At this point, the elemental is trying to take over, and if reason is not strong enough to prevent you from being taken over, you are in danger of being enslaved by your desire—not to mention what's going to happen to your relationship with your colleague if you act on the elemental's urgings.

Negative elementals aren't just involved with negative behaviors and objects in the outer world; they also include negative emotions and beliefs. If at some time in your life you have created an elemental that says, "I am not worthy of being loved," this elemental will go out into the world and find someone or some situation to fulfill that wish. You have programmed this elemental to give you an experience of feeling unloved, so it's going to loop through the program over and over until you get what it thinks you desire. So you go out into the world with this negative elemental in your energy field, and it finds a person that you are strangely attracted to but don't understand why. And this person basically blasts you emotionally and makes you feel unworthy of being loved. Now, this other person may be holding another kind of elemental, something entirely different from yours. Maybe that elemental says, "I must fight and protect my vulnerability in this dangerous world. So you can be with me, but don't come anywhere near me." What you wind up with is a perfect relationship for the two negative elementals—but a terrible relationship for anyone looking for love.

Elementals and childhood wounding

As I mentioned before, a negative elemental is a fixed emotion–thought pattern where desire drives thinking and subsequent actions. Negative elementals are often created in childhood. Newborn babies and young children are very connected to the soul when the ego is not yet developed. As the ego begins to develop, if the parents create a safe environment for this child, then this builds trust and the child continues to remain in connection with its soul. But when there is a break in the connection because the physical environment is unsafe or due to changes in the home that create problems for the child, then there is a loss of trust. Children can come to mistrust their parents or their surroundings, and some children can incarnate having already lost trust from experiences in another life.

There are three areas where wounding can happen between the ego and the soul:

1. *The Belly Center.* Woundings involving the first three chakras cause problems with the will, creating problems with our ability to do things, to act in the world. Woundings in the belly center usually cause the formation of the elementals of greed, anger and frustration. Issues of control, such as lust and emotional domination, also arise in the belly center.

2. *The Heart Center.* Woundings involving the fourth and fifth chakras lead to problems with love and relationships. The deep emotion of sorrow is a negative elemental arising from the heart center.

3. *The Head Center.* The sixth and seventh chakras of the head center involve how you understand life. The big negative elemental here is fear.

This is a convenient model to help us think about how elementals form, because we are looking at three distinct anatomical areas. In truth, sorrow can be held anywhere in the body; fear can be anywhere; anger can be anywhere. This model just helps to orient us and provides a way of tackling our negative elementals energetically.

So in early childhood, when the ego breaks away from the soul, the ego begins to look around in the world for a way to heal the missing connection. The ego builds desire and, as we've already seen, it seeks to fulfill its desire. Every time the ego goes after something outside of itself to fulfill its desire, it may feel satisfied for a short while; but soon the ego is again dissatisfied, feels that something is missing, and goes out seeking again. This process of the estranged ego perpetually trying to fill its own emptiness creates negative elementals. This is a kind of addiction, a conditioned response. After a while, the elementals you create sit in your energy field as those fixed desire–thoughts we were talking about. Each elemental pokes at your conscious mind from your subconscious, stirring up emotion. The emotion then becomes stronger and begins to influence your thinking. You get to the point that you are not reasoning with your conscious mind anymore, because this strong emotion is influencing your thoughts and behaviors.

Take anger as an example. Somebody does something to insult you, and an angry feeling arises. Maybe at first you say, "Damn! It is not me!" But if the emotion is strong enough, then that anger can start to color your thinking. Maybe you start to think, "How could they do that to me? How dare they do that? That is so disrespectful, so abusive! I am so angry!" And then you want to respond abusively, to give back the abuse you feel that you have suffered, and you feel completely justified in doing so. This is how elementals work. You say to yourself, as you are screaming at this person, "They absolutely deserve it." The anger elemental sits there laughing, saying, "I got you. I found my feeding trough. I am eating now." And all your thinking, all your vitality, all your good emotional energy is going to that negative elemental. The more you act on the elemental, the more power it takes from you. Are you following me?

The ancient people, the early Christians for example, called these negative elementals "demons" because they really do act like demons. They called the positive elementals, or virtues, "angels." In one of the holy books of early Christianity called *The Philokalia*, which means "the friend of goodness," the early Christian mystics and ascetics were writing about their experiences with elementals. These ancient people were not very psychologically sophisticated, so to them these emotion–thought and thought–emotion complexes really were demons and angels. We now know that elementals are of our own making; nobody else is creating these complexes. We as individuals make the elementals, but then they take on a life of their own. It's important to know that elementals exist individually, but they can also congregate collectively, sitting in the psychic atmosphere over different areas of the planet. We call these congregating elementals collective elementals.

Think about this for a minute. We recognize that each country has its very own sociocultural energy; this energy is a cultural elemental attached to the entire country. The cultural elemental attached to the United States is very different from the cultural elemental attached to Germany or China or Sweden or Brazil. The cultural elemental where you live makes it harder for you to change those particular energies, because collective energies are very powerful. Anyone who goes, for example, into a place where there has been heavy fighting or atrocities of war can sometimes feel an energetic heaviness in that area. This heaviness comes from the collective elementals that were formed at the time of the conflict. In the same way, you can go to holy sites that for many hundreds of years people have honored as sacred, a place to pray. Positive elementals are strong at these places. At these sites, you can feel a wonderful energy, and a special feeling of peace, love, or healing is often experienced there. The energy of positive elementals feels so much better than the energy of negative elementals.

Developmental stages of negative elementals

Negative elementals go through four stages of development, progressively getting worse at each stage. These stages are *attack, dialogue, addiction,* and *domination.* Let's look at some examples of each of these stages and strategies we can use to prevent our energies from being drained by a negative elemental.

Stage 1: Attack

Say you are driving down the road in your car, you are feeling good, and nothing bad is happening. Then, quite suddenly, you feel attacked by an angry thought. Something happens to make you angry, some experience in the outer world. Maybe somebody honks at you or cuts you off or even causes you to be in an accident. An anger elemental has been sitting in your subconscious, just waiting to come out and feed on your energy, and now it has an excuse to do just that. The elemental first appears to you as an angry thought. When that angry thought arises, you can choose to ignore it; you can ignore the angry feelings that set off the thought. If you don't think about the angry energy, the anger elemental will generally begin to weaken and go away.

How do you ignore an elemental? You just ignore it! You put it aside, saying to yourself that it is not important. You focus your attention on something else, something more positive. You do something constructive, think of something pleasant, or you can think of another problem you have—anything but this negative elemental you are being attacked by. Seriously. To feed or not to feed an elemental is your decision. When you decide not to give the elemental that is attacking you any energy, it will withdraw. The longer you keep your attention on this negative feeling, however, the quicker and larger it's going to grow. If you have to, tell yourself that this elemental is a demon—because it really is! If you can ignore the elemental's attack, you will deprive it of the energy it needs to keep feeding.

Stage 2: Dialogue

What happens if you don't ignore the elemental's attack, and you start to listen to it a little bit? You enter the second stage, dialoguing with the elemental, which takes a little more of your energy. Maybe the elemental says to you, "You should be upset!" If you ask it why, the elemental will give you plenty of reasons: "Because that so-and-so did this and that," and so on. When you try to reason with the elemental, saying "But they didn't mean to do it, they're normally good, they don't always act this way," the elemental says, "No, you don't really see what is going on." An elemental can be a very convincing, very tricky little demon. Elementals use your own intelligence against you. At this stage, an elemental might say to you, "Don't you remember when they did that incredibly disrespectful thing to you?" And you'll say, "Ah, yes, I remember. You are right."

So in the second stage of an elemental's development, you have an inner dialogue with yourself. You begin to dance with the elemental. You have not yet physically acted on the elemental's desires, but you have started to believe the elemental might be right. You have to use your rational mind, your reason and objectivity, to distance yourself from this elemental. Maybe your higher reasoning says, "Now, wait a minute. Let's cool off. Let's try to understand this." Maybe your soul awareness intervenes and says, "Wait a minute. What is this about? It is not you. It is a reflection. Look at yourself." Then you may have a chance to break out of the dance. One way to do this is just to visualize a part of yourself as this angry person. You are not only you but also this angry person inside of you. Once you've created a negative elemental, it operates with a kind of feeling, a kind of movement, a kind of texture, a kind of form, a kind of intelligence. It really is like a separate being with a mind of its own, and you have to dialogue with it in a positive, rational way.

The basic process for dialoguing positively with an elemental is this: You can look at this angry part of you, and you can say to it, "I am not you. You are not me. I created you for a reason." Now think to yourself why you created the elemental. You might say, "I created you in order to mistrust people and protect myself from further hurt, but I don't need you anymore. I don't need your services. It is time to let you go." Then you can call on the archangels, or whoever you look to for spiritual support, to transform the negative elemental's energy into a positive virtue. You can sense where you feel the connection to the negative elemental in your body, then cut the cord.

Stage 3: Addiction

What happens if you cannot break away from the elemental at the second stage of its development? Deeper trouble. You go to the third stage, which is *addiction*. At this stage, say you are in your car, thinking negative thoughts, angry thoughts, and you've been dialoguing for a while with the angry elemental, so finally it says, "When are you gonna do something about this appalling situation?" And then you might go to the person you see as having caused all the trouble and shout at them or say something really nasty to them. You may feel like congratulating yourself, but what you have done is acted out the elemental. The negative elemental has now been born into the world. For a short time this feels good to you. It gives you a little satisfaction, because you have expressed the elemental's anger and you feel justified in having done so. But know this: Any time you feel that you are justified in doing anything—when you say "I am right, and you are wrong"—then an elemental has gotten the best of you. This is especially true in the case of relationships. It's as if the partners' elementals are joking and laughing, saying, "They think that they are troubling each other. They don't even know we are behind the scene." So, at the third stage you start acting out for the elemental, which is now pulling your strings, and you're addicted. You have literally manifested the elemental, so you believe what it tells you even more strongly. Your energy is more and more bound up in the elemental, and it starts to gobble you up.

You know, it is very interesting that the early Christian mystics and church fathers still held a very high energy vibration, a deep connection to oneness and love; but after the Christian church was formalized, the level of consciousness dropped. These early church fathers and mystics taught that you are not connected to a sin until you have acted out your demons; this is very different from today's notion that thinking about sinning is as bad as actually doing it. In Eastern religious teachings, they say you create karma through your actions, not your thoughts. There is a very big difference energetically between the second and third stages of elemental development, between having an inner dialogue with the elemental and actually manifesting the elemental in the physical world. The amount of your energy being used up by the elemental is far greater at the third, addictive, stage.

I am sure all of you know what it feels like to get angry, then cross over into acting out on that anger. At first you feel good, because you believe that you are right. This good feeling, however, is followed by confusion and misunderstanding, which inevitably leads to a feeling of isolation and sadness, sorrow, regret, guilt, or helplessness. And then you might say, "I am sorry, I didn't mean it." You may go into this really deep pain with a sense that you have destroyed something, cut a connection, or created a wound. When this happens, you find that you just cannot communicate. Not fun. And all of this is depleting your energy. The elemental is sucking it out of you.

When you have already reached the third stage of acting on an elemental, you are in much deeper water and it is more difficult to break away from the elemental. You have to do inner work to break the connection. You are addicted to your own fixed patterns, your weaknesses. At the third stage, you keep doing what you did at the second stage to arrest the elemental's feeding, but it's so deeply rooted now that you have to go even deeper to discover the elemental's source. Did it come from your family? Why is this elemental sitting in your energy field? Until you have done this, you cannot cut the cord connecting you to the elemental to discharge its energy. As with a noxious weed, sometimes you have to keep working at it before it is completely eradicated. Later, we'll look at a male–female energetic healing process that you can use for this purpose.

Before we go on to the next stage, I want to clarify something. I am not saying that anger is always wrong or fear is always wrong. If you are standing in front of an oncoming train and you are afraid, I don't think you should be trying at that moment to cut that elemental lose—you should jump out of the way! The key is your intention. You can be angry about something and use that anger to constructively change your life; but if you keep blaming other people, you are just wasting your energy and avoiding the truth about your behavior. It is perfectly okay to say to yourself, "I don't like what's going on." But if you choose at this point to say, "It's everyone else's fault, and I am a victim of this and they must pay," then your negative elemental is dancing with joy. And the more you believe this, and the longer you believe it, the more difficult it will be for you to cut the cord. Still, at this late stage, you can still reverse the damage and transform the negative elemental. However, if you are satisfied with what you are doing at the third stage, the elemental may reach its fourth and final stage of development.

Stage 4: Domination

The difference between the third and fourth stage is a matter of volition and degree. At the third stage, although it is very difficult, you still can choose to reverse the damage and break away from the elemental. At the fourth stage, however, your volition is gone; you are dominated by the elemental. This is truly like being possessed by a demon. This stage is typically so bad that you become self-destructive or destructive to others in a way that involves a psychiatrist or even the police. To give you a sense of the progression to the fourth stage, let's look at the four stages of development of the anger elemental again.

1. Angry thoughts arise in your mind, but you are able to ignore them. The elemental may cause you some frustration and impatience, but it soon leaves you.
2. You become angry and start fantasizing about what you're going do. You are dancing with the elemental, dangerously flirting with it.
3. You begin acting out the anger, shouting angrily, saying nasty things, criticizing or threatening others, and maybe hitting them "a little bit." You still can act to reverse the elemental's damage, although now it is extremely difficult to do so.
4. Your behaviors are increasingly violent. You smash whatever is in your way, destroying things, and whoever is around you had better run for cover because you feel like killing them. You are possessed by the elemental. Even if you know you shouldn't act on it, you can't help it. You have completely lost control. This is a very dangerous stage.

As you can see, the more you advance from the first stage in an elemental's development to the last, the more extreme your behaviors become, the more consumed you are by the elemental, and the more likely outside intervention will be required. Take the elemental of sorrow, for example. The first stage is sadness, the second stage is grief, the third stage is depression, and the fourth stage is self-destructive urges or even attempting suicide. This is the progression of a negative elemental, whether it's anger, sorrow, fear, or any other negative emotion. When you get to the fourth stage, the elemental's energy is so intense that you cannot get away from it without someone else taking charge and breaking the elemental's hold on you. Maybe you will be sent to a psychiatric hospital, where you are pumped full of drugs that knock you out and actually give your mind a break from thinking about the elemental. This effort to treat an imbalance of your brain chemistry serves to distance you from the negative elemental. For a while you are able to rest, and then you get back to life very gradually. After some time, hopefully—if you really try to understand yourself and what has happened with the elemental—you can turn it around and begin to go in the right direction.

You can use deep therapy, rituals, and energetic methods to help you transform a fourth-stage elemental, but you really need to surrender to Spirit. One reason Alcoholics Anonymous has been of great benefit to people who have problems with alcohol is that it is based on spiritual principles, and ultimately they have to surrender to a higher power to get help with their addiction. Medicines are useful to get some distance and relief from an elemental in the short term, but if you don't understand the developmental process and won't surrender to a higher power for healing and support, you may not be able to get out of the destructive cycle. This is true of relationships, too. Sometimes couples get caught in mutually destructive elemental patterns that end in tragedy with deep regrets.

When you get deeper into an elemental, the elemental grows so much that it encapsulates you. For example, if you are encapsulated by a depression elemental, all you can see is depression. The spiritual healer Daskalos told many stories about people possessed by heavy, very obsessed elementals that they actually carried with them when they died. Elementals can be so strong that they can tie a person's spirit close to the Earth plane after death. If these elementals are not transformed and cleared, they can even follow family members for several generations, reappearing and manifesting in family systems. Let me tell you a story that illustrates this.

Once I was invited to do a seminar in Brazil, and we were staying with the family who invited us. It was a very wealthy family with two daughters. You cannot imagine the wealth. The house was like a castle. Fence around the house, guard dogs that would kill you. The other daughter had inherited a big radio station, and she was living in a similar house. The first night we were there, we had just flown from Atlanta to Brazil, so we went to bed early. I said to my wife, "I'm so happy that I am in bed. It was such a long flight." And maybe an hour after we had gone to sleep, I woke up. Suddenly, outside in the hallway, I heard a door open and slam, and then I heard footsteps. I said to my wife, "I can't believe this," but she told me not to worry about it, just go back to sleep. So finally I got to sleep. The next morning at breakfast, we were sitting there, and I was talking with this daughter who owned the house. "How did you sleep last night," she asked. I said, "I would like to say 'well,' but we heard some noises. We were concerned. Do you know what it was?" "No," she said, "but I was hoping that you would look into what is going on. I have been hearing it since my mother died three months ago."

Keep in mind that the mother was the one who had all the wealth. I agreed that we'd try to do something that night. So before we went to bed, we went to the cabinets in the hallway to see if there was anything there. I really had no idea what to do, and I didn't know what would happen. When the daughter opened the cabinets, we found a lot of the mother's jewelry. We all closed our eyes, and very soon I saw the figure of a woman. I described the woman to the daughter, and she began to cry. "That's my mother," she said. Telepathically, I tried to find out from the mother what the problem was. The mother said, "I am really worried, because what you don't know is that my daughters are fighting over my wealth. I am not so concerned about them, but I do care about my grandchildren, and I want to make sure that they get what they need." So I asked the woman what she wanted, and I told her daughter what she said. And the daughter really understood that she had to stop fighting with her sister and that they had to honor their mother's wishes. It was clear that the mother's elemental of worrying about her grandchildren was keeping her spirit near the Earth plane. I stood holding the daughter's hand, and I said to her, "Your daughter is here. Let's connect, and it's going to be okay. She will honor your wishes. Please go with peace." And so the mother's spirit left, and the noise didn't come back. The energy of the elemental had been transformed.

So the good news is, you can discharge the energy from a negative elemental and transform it into a positive virtue. You do this by taking the negative elemental's energy, intentionally making a new choice, and building the corresponding virtue—a thought–desire, a positive elemental—from the negative fixed desire–thought. Essentially, you first use your mind and heart to visualize something positive and constructive that you want to create, and then you take active steps to create it. Said another way, you can turn your demons into angels. The early mystics believed that there are many ways to deal with demons (sometimes called deadly sins by the church fathers), and they taught that each of the sins could be transformed into a virtue. This is the same thing as transforming a negative elemental into a positive one.

There are nine major negative elementals that we are concerned with. Any time a negative elemental is bothering you, one of these nine is probably at work. As you identify which elemental is active, you can intentionally transform it into its respective positive elemental:

1. Anger transforms into peace.
2. Pride transforms into humility.
3. Deceit transforms into honesty and truthfulness.
4. Envy and jealousy transform into satisfaction and gratitude.
5. Greed transforms into abundance.
6. Fear transforms into courage.
7. Gluttony transforms into sobriety.
8. Lust and possessiveness transform into spiritual surrender.
9. Laziness transforms into right action and love.

Developmental stages of positive elementals

As with negative elementals, a positive elemental goes through four stages of development, but this time it gets progressively better at each stage. The positive stages are *idea, dialogue, action,* and *manifestation.*

Stage 1: Idea

First, you have an idea that excites you. This idea is positive; it is good. Maybe it's the thought of a new job and an improvement in your finances, or maybe it's about your partnership, a special vacation, your physical health or spiritual development. Whatever it is, you know you'd really benefit from doing this particular thing. And you say to yourself, "Oh, that is really nice. That would be great for me." But then you may say, "But I don't think it would be possible for me to do it." So all your negative elementals start chattering, trying to convince you that you can't do it. What do you do? You just don't listen to them. You must ignore them because, if you abandon your idea at this first stage, what happens? Nothing.

Stage 2: Dialogue

At the second stage, the thought comes again, and it says to you, "Yes, it is possible. You can do it. You feel the power, and you have the ability. You can make it happen." This positive idea, this creative impulse, comes from your soul, from your higher self, into your personality. At the second stage, then, you begin to dialogue with your higher self (or perhaps your guardian archangel), and you get excited. There is something in you, deep inside, that says "Yes!" and then your whole being starts to say "Yes! Yes! Yes!" At this point, you move to the next stage.

Stage 3: Action

At the third stage, you begin to put the positive thought into action. At first it may be a small step. Perhaps you make a phone call or do a little research, or you say something to a friend about your idea: "Wouldn't it be cool if I could do that?" And your friend may then say, "Why not? I think it would be great! Go for it!" Suddenly, the idea starts getting more energy, because you are building it and you are starting to put the idea into action. The positive elemental is now in its third stage of development. It has become an inspiration, a motivating drive. You feel courage about it within yourself, and you are taking steps to realize your dream. This leads to the fourth stage of development.

Stage 4: Manifestation

At the fourth and final stage, the positive elemental begins to manifest in the world. Your dream— something that you chose to build intellectually, emotionally, physically, and spiritually—is beginning to come true. At this point, the positive elemental takes on a life on its own, just as the negative elemental did, but it is moving you in a positive direction. Rather than depleting your energy, the positive elemental carries you along on a wave of creative energy. Unlike with the negative elemental, this process is enlivening and inspiring. Because you consciously chose the direction the positive elemental would take, you are vibrantly involved with its unfolding.

So, this is the progression you will follow to create a positive elemental. You'll start with a vision or thought or idea, dialogue to build excitement and energy around it, start to act on it, then fully manifest it. Thought, feeling, action, manifestation. As you bring more and more energy, more life-force, to the positive elemental, it will begin to lift your consciousness to a higher state. This is an energetic process involving your entire chakra system.

Levels of Human Consciousness

Energy level 20	Shame
Energy level 30	Guilt
Energy level 50	Apathy
Energy level 75	Grief
Energy level 100	Fear
Energy level 125	Desire
Energy level 150	Anger
Energy level 175	Pride
Energy level 200	Courage
Energy level 250	Neutrality
Energy level 310	Willingness
Energy level 350	Acceptance
Energy level 400	Reason
Energy level 500	Love
Energy level 540	Joy
Energy level 600	Peace
Energy level 700–1000	Enlightenment

As adapted in Jones, Marie D. (2008), *2013: Envisioning the World After the Events of 2012*, p. 82.

The groundbreaking book by David R. Hawkins, *Power vs. Force*, details the various levels of human consciousness from the lowest level of shame to the highest levels of enlightenment. Each energy level is assigned a numerical range. Through many years of study and calibrations in kinesiological testing, Hawkins was able to identify well recognized sets of attitudes and emotional states and assign to each state of consciousness a number from 20 to 1000 using a logarithmic progression similar to how earthquake magnitudes are calculated: level 300 is not twice the size of level 150, but 10 to the 300th power. This demonstrates that a small increase in the power of positive life energy can result in a large increase in consciousness.

Looking at Hawkins' progressions in levels of human consciousness, it is interesting for us to consider that the energies of levels 20 to 100—shame, guilt, apathy, grief, and fear—are reminiscent of the attributes of victim energy and emotional behaviors. Desire (125) and anger (150), when used in a negative manner, correspond to abusive reactions, and pride (175) corresponds with a key attribute of rescuer behavior. All states below 200 are considered states of force, or what we might consider to represent negative elementals. We might consider all positive elementals as existing from 200 and above.

The human race, as a collective consciousness, is now at the 207 energy level. Hawkins finds that, at energy level 200, a critical change in consciousness takes place that moves humanity out of the vibration of fear and into courage. At level 500, the motivation of love and creativity comes into expression, and from 700 to 1000 (the level of enlightenment) we find the various enlightened beings or avatars. Hawkins suggests that one enlightened being at the 700+ level could counterbalance the collective negative energy of millions of lower-vibrating individuals. This is consistent with Eastern teachings brought to the West in the last half century.

Considering all of this, can you now see how powerfully and positively you might impact not only your own life but the lives of your children, your partner, and your fellow human beings by holding the most positive, life-affirming intentions and positive elementals you can in your thoughts, your feelings, your actions and behaviors?

The Nature of the Chakra System

Now we'll turn our attention to the chakras—what they are and why they are important in our development and healing. In Sanskrit, the word *chakra* means "wheel of energy." A chakra is like a central point of energy governing a certain part of the physical body. There are nine chakras in all, but for our purposes we will only concern ourselves with the first seven. These chakras, or energy wheels or vortices, exist in the etheric body, the first layer of the human energy field we know as the aura. The etheric body is in immediate contact with the physical body and connects it with the emotional and mental bodies. As shown, negative and positive elementals are lodged in these energy bodies.

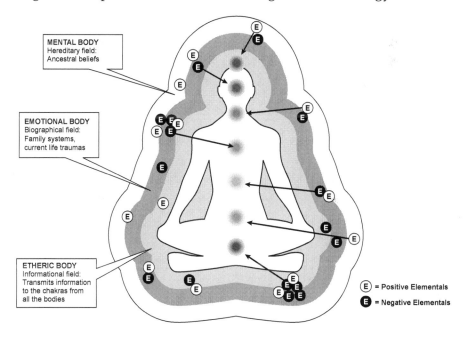

In the center of the seated figure, you see the chakras 1 to 7, with the first at the base of the body and the seventh at the top of the head. This is the physical level of the chakra system. Moving outward from the figure, the second level is the etheric body. This body is connected to all the other bodies; it is the informational field that transmits information to the chakras from all the bodies. The next level, the emotional or astral body, holds a lot of biographical experiences—your current life experiences, your family system, and various life traumas and karmas.

The final level, the mental or causal body, carries ancestral beliefs and past-life patterns.

For now, think of the physical, emotional, and mental bodies. These bodies vibrate at different frequencies, from slow to fast. Moving outward from the physical body, which vibrates so slowly that we have no difficulty perceiving it, the emotional (or astral) body vibrates faster, and the mental body is vibrating faster still. When you hear people speaking of "higher" and "lower" bodies—and even of divisions within a particular body—this is really a way of labeling a continuum of energy frequencies from slow to fast, from denser to more refined. For example, the lower mental body is our memory bank. The higher mental body is connected to the universal memory bank, to the soul. Each energetic body, including the physical body, is really a part of that super-substance we call *mind*. The physical body, sometimes referred to as the "bodymind," is just a more condensed form of mind. The emotional body is a little less dense than the physical body, and the mental body is even lighter.

Think of the different states of the element H_2O: water. The most dense form of water is ice, followed by its less dense liquid form; finally, in its least dense state, it becomes water vapor. Analogously, these states within ourselves are the physical, emotional, and mental bodies. All three bodies are under the domain or control of the soul, which is of an even finer nature and sensibility. The soul uses the three bodies as instruments of perception: the physical body is sensation, the emotional body is feeling, and the mental body is thinking.

Chakras and energetic messaging

The physical, emotional, and mental bodies communicate with each other through a fourth body, the etheric body. To understand how the etheric body works, consider the organs within the physical body. How do these organs communicate with each other? We need blood and a circulatory system to carry food, oxygen, and information to all our organs and cells. But if we didn't have connective tissue, our organs and everything else in our bodies would not be held in place and we'd wind up being shapeless and structureless. So this connective tissue surrounds everything, even our muscles, and acts as a transport membrane between the blood and all our cells. In a similar way, the physical, emotional, and mental bodies communicate with each other via impulses passing through the etheric body; the information shared between them is mostly in the form of positive and negative elementals.

The etheric body is concentrated along seven information bridges—the seven chakras. The chakras exist not only at the physical-body level but at the emotional and mental levels as well. On the emotional and mental levels, the chakras hold the elementals and the information for what we call the personality. Information is moving in both directions, much like our nerves radiate out from the spine, the center of our nervous system, to sensors in the skin and then relay information about our external environment back to the spine and brain. This is a marvelously complex energetic exchange. For example, when you smell a good meal being cooked, you might feel pleasure and delight at the thought of eating it. Simultaneously, a message is sent to your stomach, which starts to growl and sends a message back to your brain. You and your stomach are both saying, "Let's go eat!"

In a similar way, you have messages coming from the higher mind attempting to make their way all the way down to the physical body. These messages constitute the different virtues like love, faith, humility, and compassion that your soul wishes to express in the physical world. At the level of the lower mind, too—in the causal body where we store our memories from this life and other lives—the messages are coming from both directions. These memories affect our lower bodies—emotional and physical—and, therefore, our behaviors.

Say as a young child you experience some trauma or difficulty. This experience is held as a memory in your causal body. It also leaves traces in your emotional body and, at the cellular level, in your physical body. Because traumatic experiences are painful, most of us avoid thinking about them; often these memories are retained subconsciously, outside of conscious awareness. But whenever you are exposed to circumstances, environments, or relationships that remind you of that initial experience, the information has to be communicated somehow. It finds those memory banks and signals you with a warning: "Don't have anything to do with this situation. Run away!" The circuit, the channel, for these signals is the etheric body and the seven chakras.

Chakra functions and elementals

Before you can access your subconscious memories and clear the negative elementals held in your energy field, you must activate your chakras. It's important to understand what you are likely to find when you do this, so let's explore how the seven chakras function and what kinds of elementals each of them typically holds.

Think back to the developmental stages of elementals. Elementals "work" on three levels. They have a mental component—a thought or belief—and they also express themselves emotionally and physically. For example, maybe you have the entrenched belief, "I am always hurt by others." This belief may be expressed on the emotional level as anger, then escalate to your taking some action on the physical level that results in your belief being reinforced.

As long as an elemental only causes you to feel or think negatively, normally you won't cause too much damage. But, sooner or later, the negative elemental will convince you to act on those thoughts and feelings, and then the damage can be extensive and far more difficult to correct. If you dialog with a negative elemental long enough, you will start to believe what it's telling you and act on that belief. By acting out the elemental, you bring it to life in the three-dimensional world. Worse, as more people physically react to the elemental, it actually becomes a part of the Earth.

If you travel to a place where something terrible has happened in the past, like a concentration camp, you can literally feel the enormous fear, the terror, and the monstrosity. There are places like this everywhere, in every country. The heavy, palpable negative energy in these places comes from the elementals that were created there. Some elementals are collective and others are personal. Elementals can hang around for a long time. Once elementals are given life, they want more energy, more life. They attach to our energy centers, our chakras, and feed on our energy.

What is very important to understand is that elementals vibrate at the frequency of different chakras. For example, if you have elementals in your root chakra, they will likely involve survival issues—money, safety, food. Because the chakras vibrate at different frequencies, each chakra can contain a different kind of elemental. All the chakras and their respective elementals constitute your subconscious mind. These elementals sit in the chakras like little sleeping monsters. Sooner or later, in order to recharge their energy, they gradually draw your attention to what they want.

Let's look at some of the major elementals and how they function in the chakras. For each of the seven chakras, I list the chakra's psychospiritual domain, the negative elemental we will discuss, its associated elemental thoughtforms, and the part of the physical body the elemental affects. See if you recognize which may apply to you.

First chakra: Root

Psychospiritual domain
Self-Image

Negative elemental
"I am unworthy to exist."

Positive elemental
"I am abundant and secure in my physical/material life."

Associated elemental thoughtforms
"I don't deserve love."
"I'm too poor to be accepted."
"I can't let you know me, because if you did, you couldn't love me."
"I'm ashamed of who I am."
"I'm unable to love."
"The universe has forgotten me."
"No one accepts me for who I am."
"I'm always misunderstood."
"No one respects me."

Associated body parts
Reproductive system, gonads (ovaries, testes)

The *first chakra*, the root, is located at the base of the spine, the part of the spine we call the coccyx. The root chakra element is earth. Any problems in the legs or feet are related to root chakra problems.

The root chakra begins to register memories very directly in the early childhood period between birth to three years of age. What's the most important focus of life for a young baby? Safety and consistency of biological nourishment coming from the parents—especially the mother. The first three years are critically important and foundational for the rest of our lives. That's why, unfortunately, when people go into therapy later in life, they mostly blame their mothers. (Poor mothers... they raise their children, love them, and then they get blamed. A mother has to be a mother her whole life, even after her child has grown up. There is no escape.)

So, the core issues of this root chakra are *survival, safety, security, self-protection* and *instinct.* Everything is about biological function and maternal love. One of the most important ways to help keep a child's first chakra connected to the authentic self, what I sometimes refer to as the spirit-soul, is for the family—the mother especially—to offer the child adequate and appropriate physical touch and reassurance. It's important at this stage not to shame the child. Unfortunately, many people respond to the inappropriate behavior of young children by blaming them. Rather than saying "no," then gently guiding them away from that activity, they yell: "Why did you do that? Don't ever do that again!" Just that quick, the child is shamed. Even when there is general stress in the household and the child had nothing to do with it, the child can feel responsible for making something terrible happen. At this early developmental stage, children are not focused on the outer world as separate from themselves and have no conception of a universe external to them. Everything is "me, me, me!" Until the age of three, children think and feel like they *are* the whole universe. So if something terrible happens, of course they are going to internalize blame—and this does not just happen at the physical level.

In the classical view of psychology, it is believed that our picture of the world is assembled on the basis of sensory perceptions. It is said that everything that is in the mind must have first been in the eye. Today, leading psychologists, psychiatrists and consciousness researchers are discovering that this is not entirely true. At times, our consciousness is informed by non-sensory, so-called transpersonal elements. According to Ervin Laszlo (*The Chaos Point*, p. 89), "the entire sphere of mind and consciousness forms a subtly but effectively interconnected whole."

We now know that children in the first three years of life are exquisitely sensitive to elementals. They are very aware of the elementals their parents are holding because they feel the parent's moods and sense etheric energy. Maybe a child's parents never talk about their problems, and perhaps they are not even aware of their own elementals, but the child will pick up on this energy. Say a mother is very upset about something, very sad or afraid. If she starts changing her child's diaper in an automatic way, rather than gently and with focus and love, then the energy of her negative feelings carries into her baby's aura. The child begins to assimilate the energy and, at some level, comes to a decision about the energy received.

One of the big elementals that is assimilated into the root chakra is a feeling of unworthiness. This chakra is very important to one's basic sense of self-worth. I had a patient once who was convinced that he was a devil. He was not a devil, of course, but he was afraid that something was very wrong with him. As if to prove he was cursed, he said, "Look! I was born with a big mole on my back." To help him discover where he got this idea, I took him through a regression, and we went into the root chakra. He recalled a time when he was very young, maybe three or four. Any time he misbehaved, his mother—who happened to be mentally ill—would look at him with anger, frustration, and fear. She would say to him over and over, perhaps thinking it would make him behave, "You are acting like the son of Hitler!" At the age of three or four, my patient didn't understand what his mother's comment meant, but he saw the look on his mother's face and heard the fearful tone in her voice. Later, when he learned about Hitler, he made a subconscious decision that, if he was like the son of Hitler as his mother said, then he was evil. So he had to release this energy and give his mother's judgment back to her. Only then were we able to cut the cord of energy that connected him to that very big, very negative elemental.

What you hold in your subconscious is like a picture that the child inside of you has decided for some reason to tuck away, but it's still there in your energy field, impacting you as an adult. I had a very funny experience when I was four years old. For most of my life, any time I ate chocolate I would have a bad reaction to it. So I went into a regression and saw myself at my fourth birthday party. My mother had bought this big chocolate cake, and it was sitting in on the back seat of the car. It was 1954. The car door was open, and I was so excited about my birthday that I wanted to help my mother like a little big man. "I'll carry the cake!" I thought. So I took it out, and it fell on the ground. The cake broke in half. My mother came out, saw the ruined cake, and was momentarily upset with me. "Oh my God," she said, "what will people think when they see this cake?" So immediately this four-year-old child who was me got the message that other people's thoughts and feelings were more important than mine, that "How you look is important, not who you are." That's a big message.

After I dropped the cake, the rest of my birthday went fine. I had a great time, and I forgot about what my mother had said. I ate a piece of the cake, and I didn't have any problem with it. But several years after this experience, any time I wanted to eat chocolate I'd feel like vomiting. Finally, thirty years later, curious to see if I had an allergy to chocolate, I got tested. I was not allergic to chocolate. So then I did this regression, discovered the cause of the problem, and let it go. The next day I ate some chocolate without any physical reaction whatsoever. Now I can eat chocolate any time I want to—no nausea, no problem. My experience with chocolate shows that childhood events can be very powerful, even if we don't think they are such a big deal.

An elemental thoughtform associated with the first chakra is "I don't deserve… ." This can express itself in a feeling that life is not abundant, that you are poor. Oftentimes when the root chakra is wounded, people get obsessed with material possessions, thinking that they are substitute for love; or they'll get wrapped up in food as a substitute for love. In the case of food, you might not want to eat anything or you may have problems with eating too much. People can seek all kinds of substitutes for the normal feeling of safety at the root chakra level. For example, you may want to hold onto things, especially material possessions. Some people with first-chakra problems hoard objects, never satisfied with what they have but unable to let go of anything.

The root chakra also involves the physical body and a basic sense of self-worth in the physical world. Some people are not connected to their physical body, and this is also a root chakra issue. Maybe as a child you got one of these messages from your parents: "We don't want you"; "You are an accident"; "You're not my child"; "You are a burden on us because you are another mouth to feed and we don't have enough"; or maybe "You cause too much trouble" or "We wanted a boy, not a girl." So you are unable to own your own body presence. Maybe a brother or sister gave you the message that you were not wanted. Maybe they tried to drown you when you were a baby because they couldn't get enough attention once you came on the scene. Or maybe an older sibling had to take care of you and let you run off just to see what would happen. Or the family is moving all the time because of financial problems.

When a young child sees his parents having terrible fights, he may feel like he is the reason they are fighting and that it would be better if he didn't exist. This is also root chakra wounding. Some children are just not seen because there are too many other children in the family, and they are not in their bodies for that reason. As you can see, there are many possibilities for first chakra woundings.

As touched on before, the major emotion of the root chakra is shame, a feeling that "I did something wrong; I don't know what it is, but it's something wrong." Young children are very sensitive. If you laugh at something they are doing, or if they make a mistake and you laugh, this is a shame-producing experience. So what one often finds in this chakra when there is wounding is what we call the "unworthy self." This self doesn't feel valuable and struggles to survive. If you are the kind of person who struggles all the time making money and managing your finances, then the root chakra is where you need to start working.

Naturally, the root chakra is your grounding to the Earth and the physical domain. This first chakra involves your instinctual sense of how to survive, how to maneuver in physical life, how you see yourself as a physical being, and how authentic you are with others within your physical world. When this chakra is wounded, you may feel ashamed of showing your real feelings to the world and you may take on a mask, a phony self. This would be the same as the elemental thoughtform, "I can't let you know me, because if I did you couldn't love me." Instead of sharing who you really are, you might present yourself to others as someone they will find acceptable. This is an example of how elementals can develop and can be passed on. Elementals can live for a long time.

Note that the first chakra energy has a natural connection to the fourth (heart) chakra, which is involved with nurturing. A good example is a mother breastfeeding her child, giving food and love. There is an old saying, "Home is where the heart is." It is a place where you feel, or should feel, loved and receive nourishment. In the physical domain of survival, you love and care for yourself from your heart. You nurture yourself and your family from your heart. In terms of our overall development, the first and fourth chakras are probably the most significant. We now know that the neurological connections in a child's brain are being formed within the first year of life. By the end of the second year, this process is mostly finished. This early developmental period of life is very significant.

Second chakra: Sacral

Psychospiritual domain
Inner feelings

Negative elemental
"I am vulnerable to others."

Positive elemental
"I am open to emotional intimacy."

Associated elemental thoughtforms
"No one can get close to me."
"Love endangers my well-being and attracts hurt and pain."
"I feel insecure."
"It's scary to be by myself."
"I mistrust everybody."
"I don't know if I can love or have what I want in a relationship."
"It is not safe to commit to a relationship."
"No one loves me enough to put up with me."
"I can't be myself in a relationship without hurting the other person."

Associated body parts
Spleen, kidneys

The *second chakra*, found in the area of sacrum, is also referred to as the sacral chakra. This chakra involves the water element and is governed by the kidneys. The sacral chakra holds your feelings for life: your passion, desires, intimacy with others; your ability to enjoy. This is your pleasure center, and your sexuality is here. The second chakra gives you the capacity to enjoy life. It allows you to feel, taste, enjoy, and get emotionally close to others. The second chakra is also involved with how you feel about yourself and others. Located in the pelvic area, it is connected strongly to the fifth (throat) chakra. Emotion is felt in the sacral chakra and expressed in the throat.

The activation of the sacral chakra normally occurs around three to eight years of age, during the so-called magical years of childhood. The child's identity is shifting into the second chakra, which has to do with connections to and relationships with family members. Whereas the root chakra is physical safety, the second chakra is emotional trust. Normally, when a child is wounded during this period, the strongest emotion is fear and a reluctance to risk emotional intimacy. One's family is the first point of activation.

The second chakra contains the memory of traumas and difficulties as well as the pleasant and joyful experiences of childhood. When this chakra has been wounded, there tends to be issues of mistrust in getting close to other people. Some of the elemental decisions that are made during this early period are reflected in statements such as these: "I don't know if I can love or have what I want." This shows a kind of confusion about emotional connection. "I feel insecure in the relationship. I don't let anyone close to me." In this case, emotional safety is the issue. "If I love, I will be hurt." "I am weak." "I am frightened of being alone." "I can't trust anyone." The substitute for the normal feelings of passion, joy and enthusiasm that the second chakra brings are certain addictions; because, if you cannot feel a normal sense of joy and excitement and happiness, then you are likely to feel anxiety or sadness or nothing at all. The result can be an addiction that serves as a replacement for intimacy and emotions. On a scale of 1 to 10 (with 1 being the lowest and 10 being the highest), how much drama is in your life right now? If you score yourself above 5, then you have a lot of second chakra activity that needs to be healed or cleared. Your inner child needs some work. A score of 5 or less is more or less okay; you are not so in need of addictions or intense emotions to satisfy your emptiness. (Of course, your score can change depending on circumstances.)

The second chakra also has a very magnetic nature. A magnet attracts things to itself. The second chakra can pull negative things in when a person's emotional boundaries are not clear. Normally this happens because the chakra is holding a lot of old negative elementals. These elementals may resonate with, and attract, similar energies. So if the wounded child is holding a feeling of powerlessness, the boundaries are not going to be very good and the second chakra will pull everything in unconsciously. Old family patterns are then replayed. At the same time, the chakra can contain positive elementals that go out and attract good experiences as well. So both positive and negative types of experiences can happen.

The second chakra is also in large measure the beginning of our creative impulses. The creativity at the sacral level moves through the chakras to the throat, where it is expressed through communication, art, or music; through building and manifesting things. The second chakra normally has an intense nature. When it is wounded, we try to fulfill the emptiness through different forms of drama—like sexual drama, relational drama, work drama, drama and drama and drama. When this chakra is wounded, what you can feel is anxiety, fear, depression, and a heaviness over the energy center. Normally, this chakra should feel enthusiastic—the same kind of feeling that the happy child feels, a content and peaceful energy.

Combining the first and second chakras, we are talking about childhood from birth to about eight or nine years of age. Core issues during this period involve *bonding, parental nurturing, appropriate physical touch* (not too much, not too little), *self-esteem, safety and protection, boundaries,* and *emotional trust.* If the child experiences wounding or insecurity in this period, there is a tendency to feel unlovable and to have fears. School issues can start during this period, as well as sibling rivalries as younger children are born into the family. A healthy second chakra is key for intimacy in relationships.

The chi center in Chinese medicine is located in the second chakra. If you are calm, peaceful, balanced or happy, then your second chakra is open and receiving the life-force energy. If you are pulled back, shut down, and blocked in this chakra, then you are likely to feel not only depressed, but fatigued and lacking energy. Therefore, the second chakra is very important to clear.

Third chakra: Solar plexus

Psychospiritual domain
Self-Concept

Negative elemental
"I am helpless."

Positive elemental
"I am successful in all that I do."

Associated elemental thoughtforms
"I need you to do it for me."
"I can't take care of myself."
"My success depends on you."
"My survival depends on you."
"I do what I'm told."
"I must fight to succeed."
"It makes me angry to be such a victim."
"Nothing comes easy in my life."
"I feel helpless to change my life."
"I own those I love."
"Everyone takes advantage of me."

Associated body parts
Pancreas, adrenals

The *third chakra*, the solar plexus, is your power center, your achievement body. The organ that governs the third chakra is the liver. Its element is fire. This chakra affects the appetite. The third chakra is what you think about yourself, your self-esteem, which is a little different from self-value in the first chakra. Self-value and worthiness are more about your existence, just the fact that you exist; solar plexus is how you think about yourself, whether or not you feel you are successful.

The activation and focus for the third chakra usually begins around eight to eleven years of age, the preadolescent period. This chakra is the center of the will. When it activates, the magic of childhood has gone, but the craziness of the teenage years has not yet begun. At this age, children feel curious in their skin; they have long arms and legs relative to the rest of their bodies. They are focusing less and less on the family as the primary circle of activity, but school and the development of social relationships are very important. They begin also to learn how to perform, how to work and get rewarded for doing a job, but they also don't feel so good if they don't do their job.

When the third chakra is wounded, we normally find issues of control on the one hand and helplessness on the other. Normally in this phase, the biggest source of a child's wounding is parents or teachers. The child now is moving away from the magical essence of second chakra joy and good feeling. To be loved, acknowledged, and accepted requires proving oneself worthy, so the child wants to perform well in school to earn love.

Children whose third chakras are activating learn about competition. They learn how to work with their peers, cooperating together in groups, in teams, in sports. Normal social conditions begin to pressure them to perform. One of the big issues here is how the parents handle performance. One of the big problems that many parents have is that they are not very clear in differentiating between acceptable behaviors and the innate worth of the child. The child's self esteem can be badly wounded if the two are confused: "You did so bad. Why are you bad? Why are you trying to hurt us?" Statements like these shame and demean the child by taking emphasis off of the context of the performance and putting it on the child's personal worth. Children receiving such messages often feel like their self-value is permanently diminished because they couldn't perform adequately; they do not internalize the message that they can learn to improve or that somebody will support them constructively in making improvements. This leads to low self-esteem.

The self esteem of children in the preadolescent period can be wounded in other ways. Remember that proving themselves and doing a good job is how they feel loved. It may happen that parents don't encourage their child's independence. They do too much for the child, and the child becomes dependent on them. Or perhaps the parents may not offer enough help to the child, and the child doesn't know how to ask for help. So the child begins to cultivate negative elementals around the situation: "I can't do it myself." "I need someone to care for me." "I feel helpless to change my life." On the control side, the child may develop these negative elementals: "I have to fight for what I want." "People are here to serve me." "Everything is a struggle." One of the biggest third chakra elementals in society is "I am not good enough, and I will never be good enough." Another big one is "I am angry, and I am fighting for my life." This is a very dramatic solar plexus energy: "I am not worthy of respect." Or perhaps some teacher picks on the child without any reason; maybe the child just reminds them of somebody else they don't like. Teachers can also take out their anger and frustration on children by criticizing them. This is a form of abuse. In older times, when many of us were growing up, parents often assumed that the teacher was right and you were wrong. With children today, it is very different: Their parents tend to assume the teacher is always wrong.

When the third chakra is wounded or frustrated, the will is also frustrated, and this results in the emotion of anger. Any time you are feeling angry, it is likely the anger is experienced most strongly in your solar plexus, and this is a clue to look for persistent negative elementals that may have formed when your third chakra was activated. Addictions can also arise from third chakra wounding. Other aspects of the third chakra are social relationships, work values, the sense of success, and our power center—the center of our materialistic thinking process. So one type of addiction that develops from third chakra wounding is workaholism—and, of course, in Western society, everyone enables that addiction! Another addiction is always having to prove yourself or incessantly seeking out praise, acknowledgment, and recognition.

It is important for parents of preadolescent children to understand that they need adequate time to rest. Don't push them. On the other hand, you need to set clear boundaries; you need to educate them that doing well at school has value and it is okay to compete, but help them realize that their fundamental worth does not depend on outcomes. Just talk to them. Listen to what they say. Help them find constructive solutions to their problems. Maybe they need tutoring or you need to talk to their teacher. Whatever the case, be supportive of them. Don't judge them harshly if they are bad or criticize them because they didn't do well enough. Instead, give the message that their behavior or their performance can be improved, but you love them anyway. When your children start excelling or doing better, share your joy with them. It is important, however, that they are improving and doing things for themselves, for their own joy in their accomplishment, and not just for you. In this way, you teach your children real autonomy.

Fourth chakra: Heart

Psychospiritual domain
Self-nurturing

Negative elemental
"I suffer."

Positive elemental
"I am unconditionally loving."

Associated elemental thoughtforms
"I always pay a price for love."
"I'll never regain what I have lost."
"There is always something missing in my life."
"I carry the weight of the world on my shoulders."
"I feel guilty, because I can't do all that I should."
"Love always seems to bring suffering."
"It's my duty to accept the bad."
"I care more than everybody else."

Associated body part
Thymus gland

The *fourth chakra,* the heart center, is located in the chest. Its element is air. This chakra involves how you care about yourself and others. The heart chakra is the first of the chakras that extends beyond you. To review, the first three chakras are egocentric; they are the "me, me me," concerned solely with your own needs. Briefly, the first chakra is about food, the second chakra is about sex, and the third chakra is about personal power. The fourth and fifth chakras are ethnocentric, concerned with "us": your "me" plus another, such as your partner or family unit, your nation, or the group you identify with. The heart involves caring, love, unconditional love, acceptance, tolerance, and openness to accept and embrace life.

As I mentioned before, the fourth chakra is naturally connected to the first, root, chakra. Your first chakra holds the sense of tribe: who you feel you belong to, your sense of home and roots. As a teenager, tribe is the peer group you belong to, your friends. When the heart chakra begins to activate in adolescence, we have our first conscious experience of something great, something higher, something divine. This does not mean that young or preadolescent children don't have a heart—of course they do—but the more conscious focus of the heart comes in the teen years. Heart energy becomes a finer feeling. The way it generally expresses itself is when we fall in love with the idea how life should be, how our parents or teachers should be. Or perhaps we fall in love for the first time with another person—a wonderful, magical feeling that most often ends in a sense of betrayal and despair, not being able to eat for weeks, being unable to think, and in general just feeling like dying. I know all of you can remember *that* wonderful time! When you lose that magical feeling of love, or when you lose connection to the group, you experience wounding in your heart chakra.

For families with a teenager, it is best not to move at that time. A sense of place, and staying in the same place, is very important in adolescence. This is the period when teens form peer bonds, and they also go through radical developmental stages during this very rocky time. For many of them, it is very hard when they feel like they do not belong, so being a member of a stable group of peers is significant. This is a time when they focus on the opposite sex and forming relationships. Also, as anyone who has lived through the teen years knows, this can be a rebellious time. Questioning parental authority is par for the course. Rebellious teens may be fighting for a new idea, going against what they see is not perfect, or they may fight against what is accepted by the society. They may fight just to be fighting. Quite often, even though it may seem that they don't want to have anything to do with their parents, teens are also observing their parents' relationship. If it is a good relationship, most likely they will still find something wrong with it—because that is the nature of teenagers—but if they see a cooperative bond between the parents and there is love in the relationship, later they can more easily reconnect with their parents.

Let's look at some of the elementals that can develop when the heart chakra activates: "I can never regain what I have lost." "If I love, I have to sacrifice myself." "To belong, I have to fit in and do what the group wants me to do." "There is always something missing in my life." Some of them are normal teenaged feelings. One elemental that forms in the heart chakra is "I feel responsible for the world." This is a kind of a rescuer position. Others are "I am guilty" or "I must not love or I will be hurt." Classic elementals of disappointment or betrayal may arise at this time: "I must accept all the bad that comes to me in life" or "Nobody cares about me."

Most importantly, the heart chakra is the center of unconditional love. When there is wounding in this chakra, something else is substituted for the heart's normal feeling of love and understanding. Guilt may be substituted for the natural feeling of love, or a sense of duty or sacrifice may take over. You may start to think that if you are loving, then you are suffering, and therefore suffering must be a part of life. Guilt usually evolves from first chakra shame; suffering comes from the second chakra; and duty comes from the third chakra. Sacrifice comes from the fourth chakra: "I have to give myself up to be loved."

The strongest emotion that comes from fourth chakra wounding is sorrow or sadness, and oftentimes it is hidden. When you experience a profound loss, normally there are three strategies that allow you to avoid feeling the sorrow or sadness. In all three cases, there is a tendency to substitute a self image for real, authentic feelings. One way is to decide to take care of other people instead of yourself. You act like you don't need anything. This is the image of the caretaker, the rescuer sacrificing self. In this case, what you are doing is avoiding feeling that your needs are not really met. A second strategy is simply to become a performer, substituting work and performance for love to avoid feeling yourself completely. Here, the third chakra dominates, and you think you can manage to go through life without feeling the sorrow as long as you feel successful. The third strategy is to dramatize other feelings to drown out your sorrow. You amplify those feelings, really turning them up, until they become very provocative—normally in a negative way. This allows you to believe you feel very deeply when, in fact, you are avoiding feeling. You may feel very depressed or very high, but those feelings are not real. You have convincingly created them, like an actor or actress does.

Elementals created at the stage of fourth chakra activation can lead us into addictions—to suffering, to duty, to sacrifice—or to being stuck at the early, romantic phase of relationship, unable to develop deeper and more authentic feelings in partnership.

Fifth chakra: Throat

Psychospiritual domain
Self-Expression

Negative elemental
"I must lie to get what I want."

Positive elemental
"I am truthful, honest, and have integrity in all that I communicate."

Associated elemental thoughtforms
  "If I express my true feelings and needs, I will be ridiculed."
  "If I can figure out what makes people tick, I can con them into anything."
  "I must be quiet, or I will make a fool out of myself."
  "I must tell people what they want to hear, or they will reject me."
  "I do not deserve to speak up."

"I must talk constantly to validate myself."

"If I act nice enough, I can get anything I want out of people."

"I must act loving to get sex; I must give sex to get love."

"If I tell how I've been victimized, I can get pity and attention from people."

"If I act bossy enough, I can intimidate people into giving me what I want."

Associated body parts

Thyroid gland, parathyroid glands

The elements of the *fifth chakra* are ether and fire. Also known as the throat chakra, it governs the increase of willpower, your energy level, and how you express yourself.

The throat chakra, which functions to communicate, is very connected to the second chakra and to the heart. It communicates emotions, understanding, love, and the truth. It is always active throughout life, but it activates more consciously in the late teen years. Your capacity for listening is a function of the throat chakra, and so are creative expression and manifestation. The biggest problem that arises in the fifth chakra normally involves second chakra issues. If you feel like you cannot really ask for what you want in an honest and authentic way, you will have a tendency to distort the truth, to lie or manipulate for control, with your voice. This is a combination of the second and third chakras working together. When I was a teenager, I knew many masterful liars. I had a friend who could lie so well, he wasn't afraid of anything. He could lie to any policeman with a smile. This reflects chakra wounding with the elemental thought pattern, "I have to lie in order to get what I want."

When I talk about lying, I don't just mean lying all the time in a negative sense. The trickster, a common figure in many cultures and religions, represents that part of ourselves that creatively uses communication to get across points—and this can be done for good, not bad; to help, not for control. In American Indian lore, for example, Coyote is a shapeshifter. Coyote changes form to trick people, normally in a comical way, to teach them something. In the same way, when you are having a problem and ask for some guidance or sign, your trickster will often show you something humorous to help you understand the situation at a deeper level.

Many years ago when I was trying to change jobs, I was hesitant to go out on my own, into my own practice. One day, driving to work, I saw a turtle crossing the road. I stopped, picked up the turtle, and put it on the other side of the road. I don't know why I did it. Then, two weeks later, on the big four-lane highway close to my office, I saw another turtle in the middle of the road. I stopped the car, picked up the turtle, and put it on the other side. I felt like I just had to do it. A few weeks after that, I hadn't been able to make a decision about changing my job, so I went to the mountains. I stayed overnight and prayed and asked for help in deciding what would be the best thing for me to do. "If I have my own practice," I reasoned, "I can also travel more and teach more, but if I stay at a regular work situation, then I don't have that opportunity. So what am I supposed to do? Please God, give me an answer!" In fact, I already knew the answer: I should have gone long ago. But you know how you play games with yourself: "Oh, I don't know what to do!" So I was walking down this side road, still trying to decide what to do, and suddenly a dog came up and started staring at me. I petted him a little, and he started to walk along with me, and I was enjoying his company. Suddenly, the dog took off into the woods, and I missed him. I did not know the dog was a trickster. After a while, the dog came out of the woods with a turtle in his mouth, and he put the turtle right at my feet. I said, "Oh, my God!" and suddenly realized that the word "dog" in English is "god" spelled backwards. Finally I got the message that Spirit was trying to give me: "I am the turtle. I am too slow to cross the road." So I left the clinic where I worked, and six months later it closed. The throat chakra teaches us to listen to Spirit's lessons.

Sixth chakra: Brow

Psychospiritual domain
Self-Perception

Negative elemental
"I see only imperfection in myself."

Positive elemental
"I am objective, neutral, and compassionate."

Associated elemental thoughtforms
"I'm wrong; you are wrong."
"I can't do anything right."
"It's all my fault; it's all your fault."
"I can't forgive them."
"I'm defective."
"They're not good enough."
"Mistakes should be punished."
"The worst will happen."
"I'm a miserable sinner and I deserve hell."
"Society is not worth participating in."
"I have nothing to contribute to the world."
"Relationships are a trap."

Associated body part
Pituitary gland

The *sixth chakra*, the brow, governs the senses and memory. Its element is water. It has a positive effect on sleep and dreams. This chakra begins activating in late adolescence and into adulthood. It affects how you perceive yourself and your ability to understand. When the brow chakra is clouded with elementals, your view of the light is narrowed, like a horse wearing blinders.

The biggest elemental in this chakra is criticism and self-judgment. You can clear and transform all the other chakras, but if you don't clear the elemental of criticism, it will repeatedly create self-doubt. This is really a very self-destructive energy. Criticism, blame, and doubt destroy reason, logic, truth, compassion—everything. These are the most common elementals you find at the sixth chakra: "I am wrong." "You are wrong." "You are right; I am wrong." "You are wrong; I am right." "I am to blame." "You are to blame." These negative elementals are at play when you see things in terms of "black or white," with no room for shades of gray, or when you say something absolute like "I will never, ever forgive them."

The solar plexus and the sixth/brow chakra are connected. Solar plexus is the center of the will. The sixth chakra involves planning, vision, and building your life. The major elemental that attaches to both of these chakras is "I am not good enough." If you have a strong sense of superiority and pride, you may outwardly express the opposite: "They not good enough." "I am superior, you are inferior." But internally, this attitude can quickly flip back to "I am inferior; you are superior." Psychologists refer to this cycle as a vacillation between the extremes, or poles, of inferiority and grandiosity. Here we see the concept of polarity at its strongest.

Another elemental we find at the sixth chakra level is the concept of "justice," which too often means blame: "Mistakes should be punished." "You are wrong and must be judged." But blame is not justice. Unfortunately, this elemental holds a very old idea about God: the idea of a frightful, punishing god. Because sixth chakra energy is being cleansed now as we humans move toward a higher level of consciousness, the idea of this god of punishment has returned. This is an expression of the fundamentalist religious beliefs on the planet— very strong beliefs that are sometimes, unfortunately, the basis for terrorism. Often, fundamentalists are obsessed with the idea that they are right and others are wrong: "If you don't believe what I believe, you will not go to heaven." This idea can be so strongly held that it becomes irrational, a justification for violence against others. Another sixth chakra elemental, a favorite of the critical self, looks for catastrophe under every rock: "The worst is going to happen." This can result in extreme defensiveness and paranoia, which also breeds violence.

When functioning normally, the sixth chakra brings perception, intellectual and intuitional understanding, clairvoyance, and far-reaching vision.

Seventh chakra: Crown

Psychospiritual domain
Higher Purpose

Negative elemental
"I have no higher purpose in life."

Positive elemental
"My life is full of inspiration and a higher purpose for living" or "I am part of the divine plan."

Associated elemental thoughtforms
"I'm not sure what I really want."
"My life has more meaning than others.""
"My ultimate dream is the dream of my country."
"I just want to have a good time and avoid pain."
"My primary goal is to work hard and be comfortable."
"What matters most to me is a pleasant lifestyle with all the modern conveniences."
"I'll feel fulfilled if people admire me."
"My physical health is the most important thing to me."

Associated body parts
Pineal gland

The *seventh chakra's* element is fire. It represents the connection point between the physical body and the other dimensions, to spiritual worlds. Normally in the very young child the cranial bones are not fused, so this area of the crown is very soft and this center is very open. Then, as these cranial bones fuse, changes begin in the energetics.

The crown chakra normally connects us to our spiritual purpose and source of inspiration, and it brings existential meaning in life. If the crown chakra is wounded, the core elemental that forms is "Life has no meaning." When people are taught in a way that deprives them of awareness of their spiritual connectedness, they don't believe that their soul resides within them and they can't own their own spiritual experiences. Unfortunately, western-based religions like Christianity and Judaism emphasize that God is outside of you. Their teachings suggest that only a priest or rabbi has the power to give you a spiritual connection, that you cannot find this connection on your own, outside of a church or synagogue. Once only kings were thought to have a divine right to a direct connection with God, but the common folk seeking this connection were considered heretics or, at the very least, a threat to their rulers. Denying the existence of God is another way of disconnecting from Spirit and the soul. I call this state of disconnection the wounded religious child.

Sometimes people feel as if there is pressure on top of their head. This may indicate that something is blocking the seventh chakra, preventing them from coming into their own spiritual empowerment. The crown chakra can become blocked for many reasons. It can happen that critical elementals are choking off energy flow at the sixth chakra, and so you never feel the crown chakra energy. Imagine the seventh chakra as the sun. If the sky is very cloudy, you cannot see the sun until the clouds break up and move away. It is the same with the seventh chakra. When a person is depressed, quite often what we find is that the seventh chakra is blocked. In depression, people normally lose their sense that life has meaning. Once they reestablish a sense of meaning and some hope and inspiration about life, it is like something very heavy and dark has been removed from the crown chakra.

The sixth and seventh chakras are world-centric, extending beyond your tribe and nation. From the perspective of the sixth and seventh chakras, when you meet someone from another country who speaks a different language or dresses and behaves differently from you, you do not perceive them as being alien; you think "We are human beings, and we are spiritual beings." You see that we are all enlightened aspects of the divine; we are brothers and sisters in Spirit; in essence, there is no difference between us. And so all the chakras now are expressing this truth. If only your first three chakras are open and clear, then everything is about "me." If your fourth (heart) and fifth (throat) chakras are also operating, then you are not just trying to fulfill your own desires but understand that everyone has needs. You feel compassion for others, and you are willing to share. You trust in change, and you accept and respect others. You care about helping those who live in your community and your country because it is the right thing to do, and you speak out on their behalf. You begin to communicate from this higher level of energy and consciousness. And when this energy begins to move up into the sixth and seventh chakras, then all of humanity and the planet as a whole becomes your concern.

On our planet now, the higher chakras are trying to activate. If we don't work now to activate them and take seriously what we have created by following the egocentric desires of the first three "me" chakras, we as a species may not survive.

Meditation to release negative elementals

Take a comfortable, relaxed position and close your eyes. Breathe deeply, relaxing your body. Now, beginning at your feet, visualize and feel white healing light moving progressively up your body: Feet, legs, thighs, hips, pelvis, abdomen, chest, heart, shoulders, arms, hands, up your neck and into your head and face. With every breath, feel the light glowing brighter and stronger. Now, release from your mind any tension and any mind chatter about today, the future, or the past. Put it all into a ball of white light and send it away into the universe.

Now, feel the golden light of your soul, your higher self, bathing you as you lift into a column of light. Feel yourself traveling higher, and feeling more free, until you reach the garden of your soul, a place of peace, love, and healing power. When you enter the garden, ask for healing guidance and positive energy to be with you and breathe it in. Re-enter the column of light and slowly return to your physical body awareness.

Now, visualize yourself strolling in a beautiful garden or other natural place that relaxes you. Call on your spiritual helpers or whoever you look to for support to join you. This can be a spiritual teacher, your Christ self, an archangel or angel, or whoever you look to for guidance. Feel their presence and love.

Review in your mind problematic moments in your childhood or any negative memories, feelings, or thoughts that have continued to return to you in your life, especially in your relationships. Or you may choose a repeating negative or self-defeating behavioral pattern that limits you in some way as an adult. Whatever you choose, ask yourself, "Who in my family of origin carried similar negative feelings, thoughts, and behaviors that trouble and stress me in my relationships with others?" As you reflect on the answers that come to you, bring into your garden anyone from your family who was involved. Engage them in a dialogue. Tell them what troubled you about their behavior and how it made you feel as a child.

Ask yourself, "What negative feelings or thoughts did they expose me to? What role did they play in these negative encounters? Who played the victim in my family? The abuser? The rescuer?" Call on your spiritual supports to stand behind you or at your side with their love and strength. Now, tell your family that you are unwilling to carry the negative emotional burden they've given you. Show them how it hurt you and your relationship with them. Visualize and pull out of yourself the negative elemental energy they gave you. You can say to them, "I don't carry this victim, abuser, or rescuer for you any longer." Humbly, give the energy back to them and tell them they can send it back to whomever they received it from for healing, or you can give it to your guides to heal instead.

Breathing deeply, feel in your body where you've been connected to this negative elemental energy. With a sword of healing light, cut the cord that connects you in an unhealthy way to your family members and release it to your spiritual guides or directly to the light for healing. Ask for the healing light of the Holy Spirit to transform both you and those in your family. Ask the healed child within you to now appear and embrace them with your love. Observe the positive qualities in this child and, in dialogue with your family, affirm their positive qualities and receive them back into your heart. If it is possible for you to do so, exchange with them words of forgiveness and let them go to a place of healing and peace.

When you are ready, you may return from your healing journey..

The following meditation, called "The Three Balls of Light," was given by Daskalos some time ago. The aim of this meditation is to teach you how to build positive energies and reprogram your subconscious mind. Hopefully, this will attract similar vibrations to you. This is a very good exercise to reframe your subconscious mind and to feel more harmony with things. We will progressively visualize three different colors of light in our belly, heart, and head centers. With each visualization, we will do an affirmation to build positive energy. The first area, the belly, symbolizes power. The heart area represents love. The head area represents wisdom; it is the center of your intellect but also your intuition and higher knowing. We will also add a fourth ball of light, a white light above your head, to symbolize your soul and spiritual energy.

Meditation for building positive elementals

Close your eyes and breathe deeply, relaxing your body. As you relax, place your attention on your feet. Feel a beautiful healing white light flowing from your feet into your legs. Feel the light moving into your thighs, your hips, your pelvic area. Feel the light as it flows into your abdomen, your chest, and your heart. With every breath, feel the light growing brighter and stronger. The healing white light is flowing over your shoulders, through your arms, down into your hands and into your fingers. With every breath, the light expands, bringing you a feeling of relaxation and contentment. Now feel the healing light flow into your neck, your head, and your face. With every breath you breathe, it grows brighter and stronger.

Now bring your attention down to your belly area. And as you breathe, begin to visualize and feel a beautiful sky blue ball of light beginning to form in your belly. And feel this healing light growing and expanding. As it expands, repeat to yourself the affirmation, "I am peace and harmony. I am peace and harmony." Feel the sky blue swirl of light growing to fill your belly area. "I am peace and harmony." And as you breathe, feel the sky blue ball of light expanding, filling the room around you. And now repeat the affirmation, "I wish the world peace and harmony. I wish the world peace and harmony." And feel the ball of light expanding even further into the environment all around you. "I wish the world peace and harmony. I attract only peace and harmony into my life." Gently now, allow this energy to continue to grow and expand however it wants to.

Place your attention on your chest area and begin to visualize and feel a beautiful rose-pink ball of light in your heart center. And feel this rose-pink ball of light expanding through your heart and chest as you repeat the affirmation, "I am love, compassion and forgiveness. I am love, compassion and forgiveness. I am love, compassion and forgiveness." Feel this beautiful rose-pink ball of light expanding to fill the room and extending beyond it. With every breath, feel it expanding broader and brighter as you repeat the affirmation, "I wish the world love, compassion and forgiveness. I wish the world love, compassion and forgiveness. I wish the world love, compassion and forgiveness." Feel the energy expanding, the love and forgiveness, and see the beauty of the divine plan within all life.

Now gently, as this rose-pink energy continues to spread, bring your attention to the center of your forehead, your head center. And begin to visualize a beautiful canary yellow ball or swirl of light in your head center. And with every breath, feel this ball of light expanding as you repeat the affirmation, "I am wisdom and understanding. I am wisdom and understanding." Feel this bright yellow light expanding to fill the room and beyond. Repeat the affirmation, "I wish the world wisdom and understanding. I wish the world wisdom and understanding." Feel the bright yellow light expanding out to the world, and allow this energy to continue spreading.

Turn your attention now to the top of your head. Visualize a beautiful pure white ball of light floating over the top of your head, as you repeat the affirmation, "I am one with the universe and the divine plan. I am one with the universe and the divine plan. I am one with the universe and the divine plan." And feel this ball of pure white light expanding to fill the room and beyond. And repeat the affirmation, "I wish the world oneness with the universe and the divine plan. I wish the world oneness with the universe and the divine plan. I wish the world oneness with the universe and the divine plan."

And very gently begin to become aware of your feet, your legs, your torso. And with every breath you breathe, feel yourself anchoring more and more of this divine light of love into the room. And gradually become aware of your body sensations. Move your feet, your fingers, your legs. Wiggle your toes and stretch a little bit. Rub your hands together, faster and faster, then massage your face, your arms, your ears, your neck. And begin to return and awaken.

Polarities and Energy Exchanges in the Chakras

Think back to our earlier discussion about female and male qualities, the *yin* and the *yang*, and the energetic polarities—the positive/masculine and the negative/feminine. To review, each of us has certain masculine and feminine qualities and energies that we have developed in the unique crucible of our families, largely in response to our parents' energies. These energies play out in our current relationships—often subconsciously, as we have seen. In our discussion of polarities in the chakras, keep in mind that when I speak of positive and negative energies, I am not talking about good and bad. Also, remember that our roles can change in life, and the energy polarities may become reversed.

Balancing male–female polarities

For clarity's sake, we will first examine the energy polarities and how they are balanced based on traditional male–female roles and the basic gender mapping that is our genetic inheritance. This is how the polarities are depicted in the energy exchange diagrams that follow. Of course, the goal for both men and women is to find energetic balance and, ultimately, to achieve divine androgyny. Your goal in the work ahead is to balance negative and positive, yin and yang, between you and your partner as well as within yourself.

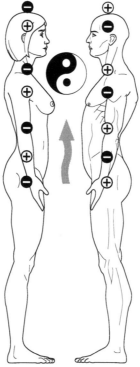

The diagram above shows how energy flows dynamically through the seven chakras of the female and male. In this simple depiction, the movement of energy between negative and positive polarities is smooth and unobstructed. Much like the poles of a magnet, opposites connect and, if unblocked, interact energetically to fuel spiritual transformation. You can think of each of these points of connection as a kind of divine energy packet, an alchemical process, a yin–yang blending of energy between the partners at the level of that particular chakra. (Refer to the energy exchange breakouts for each of the chakras.)

FIRST CHAKRA ENERGY EXCHANGE

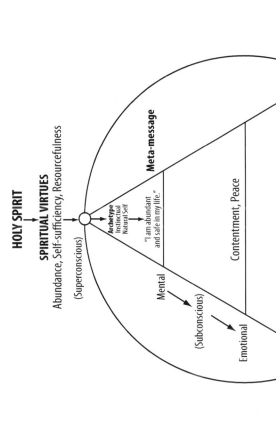

MALE
1st Chakra

Financial/material provider,
physical safety

HOLY SPIRIT

SPIRITUAL VIRTUES
Abundance, Self-sufficiency, Resourcefulness

(Superconscious)

Archetype
Instinctual
Natural Self

"I am abundant
and safe in my life."

Meta-message

Mental

(Subconscious)

Emotional

Contentment, Peace

Safety, Security

Physical
(Conscious)

DIVINE ENERGY PACKET

FEMALE
1st Chakra

Receives male energy,
offers physical nourishment,
builds nest, creates homespace

SECOND CHAKRA ENERGY EXCHANGE

**MALE
2nd Chakra**

Receives emotional nourishment and fuel, charges emotional will, recharges emotional battery

HOLY SPIRIT

SPIRITUAL VIRTUES
Attunement, Humility, Gratitude

Meta-message

(Superconscious)

Archetype
Enlightened
Lover

"I am vulnerable, open, and attuned to all life."

Mental

(Subconscious)

Emotional

Wonder, Joy, Enthusiasm, Passion

Intimacy

Physical
(Conscious)

DIVINE ENERGY PACKET

**FEMALE
2nd Chakra**

Emotional provider, nurturing, relationship-oriented, expresses affection, emotional support, interconnectedness, bonding, beautifies homespace

THIRD CHAKRA ENERGY EXCHANGE

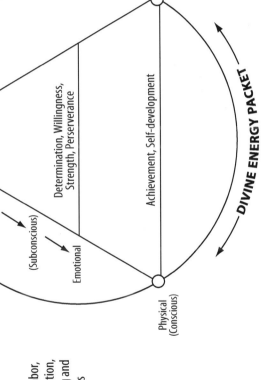

MALE 3rd Chakra ⊕

Motivated, work-oriented, success-driven, driven to achieve, build, manifest

HOLY SPIRIT

SPIRITUAL VIRTUES

Service, Commitment to Higher Ideals, Faith, Courage

(Superconscious)

Meta-message

Archetype Peaceful Warrior

"I am successful in all that I do."

Mental

(Subconscious)

Emotional

Determination, Willingness, Strength, Perseverance

Achievement, Self-development

Physical (Conscious)

DIVINE ENERGY PACKET

FEMALE 3rd Chakra ⊖

Developing the fruits of his labor, offering recognition, appreciation, acknowledgment, supporting and assisting with work efforts where possible

FOURTH CHAKRA ENERGY EXCHANGE

**MALE
4th Chakra**

Establishes stability, divine structure, order; holds space for nurturing/manifesting higher values; heart-centered decision making, fairness, mercy, justice, enlightened understanding

HOLY SPIRIT

SPIRITUAL VIRTUES
Love, Compassion

Meta-message

Archetype
King/Queen

"I am unconditionally loving."

(Superconscious)

Mental

(Subconscious)

Emotional

Acceptance, Harmony, balance, stability

Right Action, Enlightened Leadership/Organization

Physical (Conscious)

DIVINE ENERGY PACKET

**FEMALE
4th Chakra**

Empathy, love, sharing, encouragement, ethical values/ideals, family values/rituals, emotional strength, spirit of forgiveness

FIFTH CHAKRA ENERGY EXCHANGE

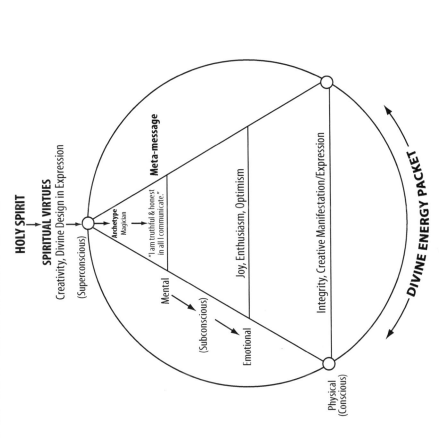

MALE 5th Chakra ⊕
Direct, commanding communication

HOLY SPIRIT

SPIRITUAL VIRTUES
Creativity, Divine Design in Expression

(Superconscious)

Archetype Magician

Meta-message

"I am truthful & honest in all I communicate."

Mental

(Subconscious)

Emotional

Joy, Enthusiasm, Optimism

Integrity, Creative Manifestation/Expression

Physical (Conscious)

DIVINE ENERGY PACKET

FEMALE 5th Chakra ⊖
Listening from the stillness of her heart

SIXTH CHAKRA ENERGY EXCHANGE

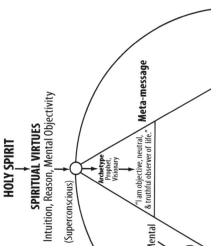
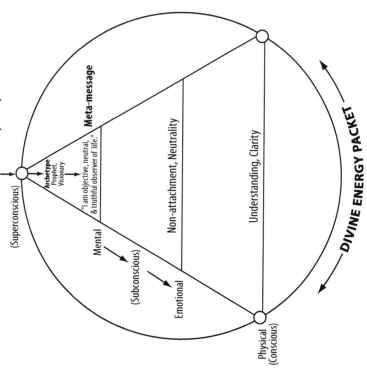

**MALE
6th Chakra**

Receives intuition, joins it
to linear reasoning to
broaden understanding,
and get "bigger picture"

HOLY SPIRIT

SPIRITUAL VIRTUES
Intuition, Reason, Mental Objectivity

(Superconscious)

Meta-message

Archetype
Prophet,
Visionary

"I am objective, neutral,
& truthful observer of life."

Mental

(Subconscious)

Emotional

Non-attachment, Neutrality

Understanding, Clarity

Physical
(Conscious)

DIVINE ENERGY PACKET

**FEMALE
6th Chakra**

Whole-brain thinking,
intuitive overview

SEVENTH CHAKRA ENERGY EXCHANGE

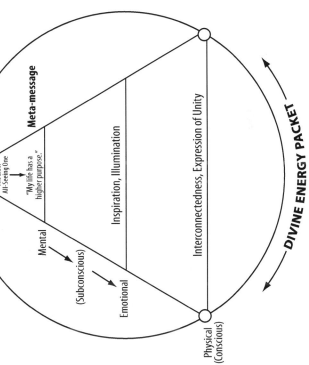

**MALE
7th Chakra**
$\oplus$

Full of higher purpose and inspiration, initiates new ideas, change

HOLY SPIRIT

SPIRITUAL VIRTUES
Wisdom, Inner Knowing, Oneness

(Superconscious)

Archetype
The Elder
All-Seeing One

"My life has a higher purpose."

Meta-message

Mental

(Subconscious)

Emotional

Inspiration, Illumination

Interconnectedness, Expression of Unity

Physical
(Conscious)

DIVINE ENERGY PACKET

**FEMALE
7th Chakra**

Builds on higher ideas and purpose, aligns and implements plans.

So, to review, *yang* is masculine and active; *yin* is feminine and receptive. For males, the *yang* energy polarity is in the first, third, fifth, and seventh chakras; the *yin* energy polarity is in the second, fourth, and sixth chakras. Alternately for women, the *yang* energy polarity is in the second, fourth, and sixth chakras; the *yin* energy polarity is in the first, third, fifth, and seventh chakras. At each chakra level, you achieve balance within yourself by learning, or experiencing, the opposite energy polarity of your partner. This happens through the exchange of information.

In couples, learning androgyny begins with the first, or root, chakra. The energy moves from the root in a spiraling fashion, through each pair of chakras, and up into the crown. For the man, the first chakra is *yang*, which means that he is very active in physically providing sustenance and safety. For the woman, the first chakra is *yin*, which is receptive of this protection and support. Now, some of you may protest that this is not true, because "I am the woman and I am wearing the pants" or because you and your partner are sharing financial burdens relatively equally. But the fact is that women have learned to take this active masculine position. The foundational female polarity is receptive and feminine. You can see, however, that as the energy moves up through the chakras, the male and female polarities alternate.

Let's look at how *yang* energy plays out with the other chakras. At the third chakra level, men are oriented toward achievement and focused on goals. The fifth chakra is also *yang* for men, and this means that his communications are direct and commanding. At the *yang* seventh chakra level, he is full of purpose, ideas and inspirations; "I have a dream" is the seventh chakra speaking. In women, the first *yang* chakra is the second chakra. This means that women are emotional providers and good in relationships. They are also emotional survivors, able to reconcile differences. The fourth chakra is also *yang* in women. Women are loving and compassionate, and they activate and initiate love and compassion in the men, too. At the sixth chakra level, also *yang*, women are very intuitive. Their thinking is more holistic , more "whole brain," while men's thinking process tends to be more linear.

We can see the energetic exchange when a typical man goes to a department store with his wife. The man would buy everything in ten minutes. He already knows what he wants to buy and is not really open to considering alternatives. The woman, on the other hand, just goes around looking at everything, taking a long, long time making up her mind before she eventually decides what she wants to buy. When you learn to balance your energies, the stereotypical male and female approach to shopping can change. I now spend a little more time exploring in shops with my wife than I used to.

What about the receptive *yin* energy in the chakras of men and women? When the energy to the chakras is not blocked, a woman's second chakra *yang* nurturing energy connects with the man's second chakra *yin*. Likewise, he receives the woman's active love and compassion in his heart chakra and experiences her whole-mind intuitive approach in his sixth chakra. Meanwhile, the woman receives the man's *yang* expression of being a good provider in her first chakra, his goal-orientation and power of achievement in her third chakra, his direct communication in her fifth chakra, and his expression of purpose and inspiration in her seventh chakra. As a couple moves together toward spiritual union, the dynamic interchange between their chakras balances their energies, and they each gain vital *yin* and *yang* energy from the other.

In the female–male diagram, you see that the movement is initiated from the man's first chakra, which activates the woman's receptive first chakra. You can think of this level as being like the traditional masculine and feminine roles: The man goes out hunting and brings home the deer, and the woman receives the deer for cooking. If this first chakra energy is blocked—if there is no deer for the woman to cook or, in today's likely scenario, no money to buy food—then the woman is blocked from taking the energy to the next level. But if the energy is flowing, the woman takes the first chakra energy and brings it up into her second chakra. Here, she becomes the active emotional provider, cooking the meal, showing affection for the family, and nurturing the children.

By nature, the man is set to receive the woman's second chakra nurturing in his second chakra, so the energy moves back to him at this higher level. If the energy continues to flow, the man brings the energy up into his third chakra; he goes out and works and achieves and builds, and he is very active. The woman receives the fruits of his effort in her third chakra, then brings the energy up into her heart for sending back to him in the form of love. The man receives this love energy in his own heart chakra, then communicates his needs clearly and directly to her from his fifth, throat chakra. And so the energy moves upward, with the woman receiving the man's communications, then taking the information from her fifth to her sixth chakra to get an overview of things. From this vantage point, she can help him to think in a broader way by sending the energy to his sixth chakra.

This is an interesting process that can lead to higher levels of inspiration. For example, say a man has made up his mind about something, but the woman wants to talk about it, to consider it from many different perspectives, to debate it. She might ask him, "Have you ever considered this or that?" She knows she has an opening to send energy to him when he finally says, "What do you think?" Then the man can take this energy up into his seventh chakra, creating new inspiration and ideas, and return it to her in the form of a larger decision, such as "This is the next step in our relationship, our marriage, our home life." This is like the divine idea. And then the whole process repeats from the beginning.

That's the traditional setup, anyway. The problem is that it doesn't usually work this way. The energy movement I've described is a natural process, but many possibilities for polarity exchanges exist. For example, if the male is not grounded or manifesting as physical provider, then he doesn't activate the female's nurturing. The result is that he doesn't receive the nurturing from her that is critical for him to feel full and satisfied enough to be able to go out into the world and achieve more. Without the energy of the man's satisfaction and achievement, the woman has little energy to bring into her heart, so she may have difficulty being loving and compassionate. Without this loving energy, he cannot communicate clearly and has trouble being creative. This is how a couple's vision and goals get smothered. The energy stagnates in the lower chakras, and neither of them have the energy to achieve a higher purpose.

Now, there are many ways this energy stagnation can occur in relationships, and we've talked about a number of them: childhood wounding, the parents' position, which one was the nurturer or provider, and what roles you and your partner learned and internalized when you were growing up. If a woman very early in life received more *yang* energy in the first, third, fifth, or seventh chakras, she can have reversed polarities. If a man is blocked in the first chakra and the woman is not receiving this flow, or if she is blocked in her fourth chakra because of wounding and elementals, then this is a limitation that creates frustration. Another possibility is that the woman may be giving her partner a lot of love, but he is blocked in his throat chakra and cannot communicate his feelings to her, so she is going crazy because she can't have a conversation with him. Energy blockages can appear on any of the chakra levels and manifest in many different ways. This creates problems. The goal is always to find balance between and within each of the chakras. No matter what the problem is, we mirror each other in partnership. This is very important to remember. You must work on yourself, and your partner must work on him- or herself. This is called self-responsibility. Once healing takes place within each partner, when you come together again, the energy can flow more freely.

Daskalos pointed to a very nice Greek myth that expresses the dynamics of this process and how, ultimately, it leads to divine union. The path to achieving androgyny, the balance between the male and female polarities, was known to the ancients. In the story of Theseus and Ariadne, you can see many of the elements of this process as it unfolds.

The Myth of Theseus, Ariadne, and the Minotaur

Theseus was the secret bastard son of King Aegeus. He returned to Athens to claim his birthright from the kingdom, because King Aegeus had no legal son. Theseus went to Athens and offered to rescue the Athenians from a contract that they had made with King Minos of Crete.

Minos had a son named Androgyny who was killed by the Athenians. We can interpret this to mean that there was a loss of unity and neutrality; the polarities were split. King Minos said that he would not conquer the Athenians, but they would have to pay for the fact that they had killed his son. King Minos demanded that every nine years— nine is the number of completion—seven virgin boys and seven virgin girls were to be sent to Crete to be sacrificed to the Minotaur. Each of the virgin boys and girls represents a male or female polarity in the chakras, fourteen in all: seven male and seven female. Equivalent to the polarities depicted in the preceding seven chakra energy exchange diagrams, these are the energy points one must balance to achieve healing and spiritual transformation.

The Minotaur (representing a negative elemental that feeds on our energy) was a very strange creature—half human being, half beast—that ate people. He lived in a labyrinth, and people who went into the labyrinth couldn't find their way out. The labyrinth represents all of your subconscious elementals. When you become trapped by your elementals, it is very hard to escape. So Theseus went to the Oracle of Delphi (symbolizing the source of the higher self) to discover the best way to kill the Minotaur. Theseus expected the Oracle would tell him to go to a great warrior and learn how to fight—an expression of the male polarity—so he is shocked when the Oracle advises him to go consult Aphrodite, the goddess of love. But he follows the advice and goes to see the goddess, and Aphrodite changes him into a handsome youth who is chosen as one of the fourteen virgin boys and girls to be sacrificed to the Minotaur.

This is what happens. As Theseus is preparing to go into the labyrinth, King Minos' daughter, Ariadne, sees him and falls in love with him. Aphrodite had woven her spell of love to bring Theseus and Ariadne into connection with each other. Ariadne doesn't want to see Theseus die, so she gives him a spool of golden thread to help him make his way back out the labyrinth. Theseus goes into the labyrinth, unrolling the thread along his path, then slays the Minotaur and follows the thread back out of the labyrinth. Symbolically, Ariadne and her golden thread serve as a spiritual guide to Theseus.

When Theseus comes back from killing the Minotaur, he starts lusting after Ariadne, because he doesn't really know her yet as a woman or what she is about. So he starts out in his relationship with Ariadne at the most basic physical level, the level of the first chakra, even though what she is offering him is a journey to divine unity and love. But Ariadne cannot be with Theseus in this way, because she has been promised in marriage to the god Dionysus. Dionysus represents the bliss we experience when we achieve androgyny within ourselves. Theseus accepts that he must find his way to a higher, more spiritual energy, so he begins the inner work of developing androgyny. Symbolically, by giving Theseus the spool of golden thread, Ariadne gives Theseus the guidance to go through the labyrinth of all of his elementals to reach his higher energy, his soul.

Having done what he set out to do—kill the Minotaur—Theseus goes home. But he forgets what his father, King Aegeus, told him before he left: "If you don't survive and the ship is returned by your men, I want to know in advance, so have them fly a black flag. But if you return victorious, fly a white flag." When Theseus reaches his homeland, he forgets to fly the white flag of victory. When Theseus' father sees his son's ship in the distance without a white flag, he is overcome with sorrow. Believing his son is dead, he drowns himself in what today is called the Aegean Sea. What this represents is that King Aegeus was very male-polarized; he couldn't accept the more female aspects of himself, so he entirely rejected androgyny. The flow of his energy was so blocked, he could only achieve divine union by merging with the more feminine element of the sea. Theseus mourns the loss of his father, of course, but through this experience he becomes more balanced within himself, his energy is able to flow, and he learns how to be a better king.

Blockages and hooks in relationships

Let's look at some of the ways the flowing energy exchange between partners is blocked. Blockage can occur when early woundings cause codependent dynamics in relationships. Let's look at some examples. Say a woman was wounded by her parents and is holding this wounding in her second chakra, so she doesn't really feel any passion or have much energy. So she might expect her partner to be her source of energy, passion, and feelings. But if his wounding is in the sixth chakra, he may say, "You have to see for me," expecting her to be his source of reason and understanding. So the attraction becomes yet another wounding, not a healthy balancing of energy. Or maybe a woman has had a very strong relationship with her father and a poor relationship with her mother, so her masculine qualities are more developed. Her polarity may be reversed, with more *yang* in the first and third chakras, so she is functioning as "the man of the house." This woman would need to attract somebody who has more female energy to balance that polarity. Maybe this man will act as mother to the children while the woman "wears the pants." You can look at yourself and your relationship to see where there may be blocks caused by reversed polarities.

Sometimes reversed polarities are the only thing that works for a while. Sooner or later, though, we learn from each other. The goal is balanced energy and wholeness. So, in time, the woman with too much *yang* will begin to assimilate some *yin* energy from her partner, and he will likewise assimilate some *yang* energy from her. This is a learning process. You are assimilating information from each other, and ultimately this brings you into balance. Whenever there is blockage, there is a need for healing because, otherwise, the relationship usually breaks down.

Energy blockages act like hooks to draw to us what we need to achieve balance so that we can grow. To see how this works, say a woman grew up with an alcoholic father who couldn't keep a job. Although she had the love and support of her mother, the family was poor and there were few physical comforts. So this woman's first chakra is pretty wounded. Her third chakra probably is, too, at least in terms of her relationship with her parents. So this woman is walking down the street one day, and the wealthiest banker in the city is approaching her from the other direction. This fellow, for whatever reason, never got any affection or validation from his mother so he lacks the experience of nurturing, but because his father was very productive and taught him to feel secure about physical things, this banker's first chakra is functioning well. But, in his heart, he has this emptiness, this craving for love. His second chakra is empty. So this man and woman are walking down the street, and when they see each other, they each cast an energetic fishing rod toward the other, hoping to catch what they lack and need to grow. The woman hooks energetically into the man's stronger first chakra, and he hooks into her stronger heart chakra. What do we call this? Love at first sight! When two people catch each other energetically in this way, it is hot, and it works very well for a while, but it's also based on codependency. This is how God and nature get us together to heal our wounds. You have got to start with what you've got.

Let's look at how our example of the woman and the banker might play out. After they hit it off, this woman soon winds up with a huge, brilliant diamond on her finger. She is living in a huge house. She has servants, and she goes out shopping with her girlfriends anytime she feels like it. The man goes to work smiling, which is unusual, and everyone is wondering what has happened to him. What has happened is that she is validating and encouraging him, so he is feeling the nurturing that he never got from his mother, and she is very happy because she feels so safe and secure. They both seem to have gotten the very thing that has been missing in their lives, so both of them are satisfied—for a while. But, as you might expect, trouble is brewing.

The couple in our example won't stay content with their arrangement for very long. Why would this be so? Because the soul keeps pressing on the personality, saying "You can't keep going this way. You've got to learn androgyny. You are here to be a whole being. You have to individuate." The personality resists, of course, but eventually something happens to give the soul what it wants. This something may look like a tragedy or a wounding, but it's actually a gift in disguise. Maybe the man gets too sick to work so, suddenly, the woman is faced with the fact that she must step in and provide for them both. So she gets a job and goes to work each day, and she learns that she doesn't have to look to someone else to provide for her. Meanwhile, the man—who has been depending on her all this time for all this affection and love—is at home by himself, not feeling very well. Soon he realizes that he can nurture himself. So their wounded chakras have been healed, and the relationship progresses. Both of them are becoming more autonomous, more independent, and now they can appreciate each other as souls rather than objects.

Let's look at some other possible relationship scenarios. Imagine a woman who has love and is also clairvoyant. She can see clearly and intuitively understand, but she lacks a feeling of power and position. She meets a man who has this power and position that she lacks, but he is disconnected from his ability to really understand or perceive higher things. Here are those hooks again: He needs the understanding and she needs the power, so they are attracted to what they need in each other. I met an older couple that exemplified this situation. The woman was a medium, and a very good one, but her husband had no such abilities. The husband was like a real warrior, though, and he had a lot of power. The only way the wife could do a reading was if they were sitting together in chairs, with him as her grounding. She would take his hand

and then, suddenly, she would be channeling a mile a minute. It was like plugging in a radio. When the channeling was over, the man would let go of her hand, saying, "Disconnecting now." This was a codependency, and it worked. It had a purpose. But a sense of autonomy and balance wasn't being built within either of them. In cases like this, no matter how good the codependency seems, something is bound to happen to force growth.

Can you think of any hooks in your own partnership? Think about how your relationship began. What created the attraction point, the feeling that you couldn't live without this person? How might this have changed with time and circumstances? Many new couples start out by creating this overwhelming feeling of romance that sweeps them up together into its embrace. Most of us over time, due to the soul's lessons for the personality, become more autonomous in our relationship. We become more fully who we really are. All relationships go through phases where the partners sense a change, like a lack of energy or a disconnection of some kind, but this is not the end of the relationship. It happens just like it does in your own life. You go through periods when nothing is happening. Then, if you activate what needs to be activated and heal what needs to be healed, you can feel yourself moving to the next level. Ultimately you realize that, whatever happens, it is just what is going on developmentally; it is your consciousness evolving. If both partners understand what is happening, there is no problem. The problem comes when one partner resists the other's evolution. That partner may become actively aggressive about resisting the evolution. Oftentimes, this leads to separation or divorce because it becomes too difficult or too constricting for one or both of the partners to remain in the blocked situation.

In all relationships, the healthy flow of energy may get blocked at some point. Blockages can occur in any of the chakras. Say the blockage is in the first three chakras; maybe the man has no grounding or ability to provide safety and security. The result is that she feels resentment and frustration, and her ability to nurture him is not activated. The blockage could be in the fifth chakra, so the love in the heart is flowing but is not being communicated to the other partner. Or the energy could be blocked in the sixth or seventh chakra. Once all of these energy channels are opened up, then integration and the achievement of divine androgyny becomes possible. Until the blockages are cleared, however, you must do the work to identify which chakras are holding the blockages and the negative elementals that keep you from progressing spiritually.

Sometimes what happens—and this is happening more and more now—is that one of the two partners feels that there is an irresolvable blockage. There is connection and progress in the relationship up to a certain level, but then you seem to reach a plateau and cannot seem to grow any further. If your partner is content at this level, you may form a relationship with God to finish the journey, or find some other way to keep growing spiritually. You may move ahead because you can't wait for thirty years for your partner to catch up. Your relationship is still okay to the level you have achieved together; but, perhaps due to your partner's own karmic program, he or she may have a difficult time moving at your pace. If you do move on, eventually your partner will do the same—with or without you. Normally, if the two of you have evolved at least to the level of the heart, the level of "us," the rest will work out because you genuinely love and care for each other and allow yourselves to have what you need to grow as individuals. On the other hand, if the relationship is stuck at the level of the lower chakras, then everything is still revolving around "me," and this makes it much more difficult to sustain the relationship. At this lower energetic level, breakups and divorce more commonly take place. We especially have seen this in the last twenty years with ever-accelerating stress and change in the world. If a breakup does occur, one partner will then be drawn energetically to some relationship in which they can more rapidly continue their spiritual journey, and the other will find someone who is vibrating to the lower-chakra energy with its slower developmental pace.

If you and your partner can agree to work together to identify and heal any blockages within yourselves and between you, a stronger relationship will emerge and divorce becomes less likely. Some couples, of course, will decide to break up after going through the healing work, but they will do so with a clearer understanding of why and with the benefit of having helped each other clarify their respective paths. Each partner is then less likely to repeat the dynamics that soured the relationship with the next person that comes along because they will have helped each other grow. They can also support each other and make the split less stressful for any children they have together. Such couples often become lifelong friends, even as they form other relationships. This, in and of itself, is a great achievement, so working to heal your blockages is definitely worth it.

Healing blockages to achieve divine androgyny

So, specifically, how do you heal energy blockages? First you must identify them within yourself, and then you work upward from the first blockage that you find, clearing each one as you go. Clearing the lower chakras often helps clear the upper ones as well. The following chart should help clarify what kinds of energy blockages occur throughout the chakra system. As you see, these are the unconscious codependent contracts that slow or prevent your achievement of divine androgyny.

Let's say, for example, you are dependent on your partner for money, safety, a roof over your head, and other material comforts. Without your partner's support, you could not survive. This indicates that you are living your polarity in your first chakra. The goal of androgyny is to feel comfortable with both male and female polarities at each chakra. To achieve androgyny at the level of the first chakra, for example, you can learn how to manage the money that your partner gives you. You may not have to earn the money, but by managing what you are given, you heal your active and receiving chakras, and feel more autonomous. If your partner suddenly is taken out of the picture, you wouldn't be left with a big hole in your consciousness filled with fear that you can't survive. You'd realize that you can provide for your own physical safety and security, even if you have never worked before. If you continue only receiving money but don't understand its value or how to manage it, then that is a big problem. It is a hole in your first chakra that needs to be healed. Look at the chart again and see if you can identify any blockages you might have in the other chakras.

Quite often if there is a stress on the system because of a lack of balance in the chakras, then a physical imbalance may appear. If you heal your wounded chakras, physical healing can take place in those organs and parts of the body that belong to the various chakras. When a chakra is wounded, it always holds negative elementals. These elementals

Wounded chakra	Key elemental	Cord	Contract or message
1st (Root)	Survival, safety	Dependency about survival issues	Save me! Keep me alive! Be my grounding. Be my physical safety!
2nd (Sacral)	Feelings, emotions	Connects to feelings and the other	Feel for me! Make me feel good! Feel with me, so I don't feel alone. Be attached to me.
3rd (Solar Plexus)	Power	Energy	Give me your energy! (Dracula effect) Let me give you my energy! I can't make it without you. You can't make it without me! I have more power than you, so I control and dominate you!
4th (Heart)	Harmony, interconnectedness	Validation	I make you feel worthy about yourself. Say yes to me! To harmonize with me is to validate me.
5th (Throat)	Communication, expression	Expressing and receiving	Speak for me! Hear for me! Say or hear only those things about me!
6th (Brow)	Vision	Ability to see	See for me! Don't see me! See only certain things but not everything! You can't see me! You are the only one that can't see me!
7th (Crown)	Inner knowing	Connection to source, autonomy	I will know and understand for you. I am the source of your understanding. You can't know and understand, I am the one who does it for you. Channel your knowing through me!

feed on your energy, so you don't have enough energy to heal yourself physically, much less activate your higher chakras. As you heal each chakra, it becomes more whole, more balanced, more defined and clear. The unconscious expression of the chakra begins to become more conscious and the qualities of that chakra—the male and female, the *yin* and *yang*—come more into balance. You have the ability to express both polarities: make money, receive money; give feeling, receive feeling. There is a nice spinning flow of energy in the chakras, both within yourself and between you and your partner. This is androgyny, and when you come to experience this flow throughout the entire chakra system, you will have achieved divine androgyny, divine love.

Before ending this book with exercises to help you on this journey, let's delve into the individual chakras a little more to see how healthy male and female energies are expressed at each level and how blockages prevent further chakra activation. Remember the story of Theseus and Ariadne: At each turn of the labyrinth, the Minotaur is waiting to feed on your frustration, disappointment, and human suffering. But there is a way to escape the Minotaur and find our way through the labyrinth, back to our souls' light: We follow the golden thread of energy through the labyrinth of the chakra system—uncovering, facing, and resolving any wounded aspects the chakras may hold—until we arrive at our ultimate goal of divine love in partnership.

First chakra

First chakra blocked male

If the first chakra in the male is wounded and the flow of energy is blocked or unhealthy, this can express itself in the partnership in several ways.

If, as a result of abusive or neglectful parents, the man is in the victim role, he may carry elementals with meta-messages such as "I am not safe" or "How can I provide safety, shelter, and support?" He may be unable to hold or keep a job, so his partner may feel pressured into working. She polarizes to *yang* in her root chakra. Because she is now polarized at the level of survival, she cannot activate her second chakra to nurture him. The man may express frustration by seeking emotional nurturing outside of the relationship, or he may develop a physical or emotional disability. He may indulge in self-defeating addictive behaviors to fill this empty second chakra. The woman may come home after working all day, expecting nurturing from her partner because their polarities are reversed. If he does not provide this nurturing, she may project her frustration by blaming him or expressing her anger that he is not being a good provider. If he received sufficient nurturing from the female side of his family of origin, he may polarize his second chakra to *yang* and become the surrogate mother and nurturer, doing typically female tasks like cooking and caring for the kids. If, on the other hand the male identifies with abusive parents, he will probably transfer this abuse by withholding support from her or making first chakra domain unsafe by victimizing her.

If the man took the role of rescuer in his family of origin and has not abandoned that role, he may continue to provide a safety net for his parents with little energy or time left over for his own family. In this case, he may actually expect or make emotional demands on his partner for support. If he is playing the rescuer role with his own new family, he may give abundant physical support and a sense of safety to the family but cannot allow himself to receive emotional support from them.

First chakra healthy male

Protector, provider of physical safety and security

First chakra blocked female

If the female is blocked in receiving energy in her first chakra, whatever her partner gives her may never be perceived as being good enough. She may get stuck in wanting to accumulate material goods or become greedy or addicted to things as a substitute for first chakra fulfillment.

First chakra healthy female

Receives physical support and safety, activating care for the home space

Second chakra

Second chakra blocked female

If the woman is wounded in her second chakra, several possibilities exist for expression in the partnership.

If the woman is in the victim role because of emotional abuse, neglect, or sexual molestation, she cannot activate her nurturing energy and may not be able to be spontaneously affectionate or sexual with her partner. She may develop psychosomatic symptoms, neediness, depression, or addictions to emotional drama and negative emotional intensity to the point of hysteria.

In the abuser role, the woman may become rebellious, mistrustful, obstinate, or very conditional in response to her partner's needs. She may become emotionally demanding, manipulative, and critical without cause and may then blame her partner for not being emotionally available for her.

When in the rescuer position, the woman may overextend herself emotionally, giving too much to her partner while ignoring her own emotional needs, denying herself satisfaction.

Second chakra healthy female

Emotional provider, good at relationship

Second chakra blocked male

In the victim role, he may "guilt-trip" his partner or withdraw and isolate himself, complaining that she does not love him or acting hurt. Or he may become silent when wounded by his partner.

In the abuser role, he may complain that he is not receiving his partner's support and feel she is not doing enough, making her feel inadequate.

In the rescuer role, he may deny himself her affections by trying to match them or reject them as unnecessary for his welfare. He may project that only his own giving is important and of value.

Second chakra healthy male

Receives emotional support and nourishment

Third chakra

Third chakra blocked male

If the male is blocked in his third chakra, he may be unable to hold a job or maintain the motivation to move forward in his life.

In the victim role, he may sit in the second chakra desire body, numbing his frustration. He may become trapped in low self-esteem by abusing alcohol or drugs, or he may escape into pornography, gambling, or high-risk endeavors that are bound to fail.

In the abuser role, he may physically and verbally project blame onto his partner, expressing violence, becoming oppressive, exhibiting impotent behaviors, or telling his partner that she does not do a good enough job.

In the rescuer role, he may overwork for the family's benefit or believe that only his work efforts have any real value.

Third chakra healthy male

Driven by achievement, focused on goals, manifesting success

Third chakra blocked female

The woman in the victim role may be jealous of her partner's work load or time away from her and exhibit manipulative and emotional behaviors. Or she may simply stay stuck in the traditional housewife role of attending to home and children, but with little or no motivation for self-improvement, thereby getting stuck in low self-esteem or self-sabotaging behaviors.

In the abuser role, she cannot appreciate, acknowledge, or support her partner's achievements and may try to compete with him.

In the rescuer role, she may believe she has no time for herself, or she may give too much, overextend herself, or bend over backward to help him be successful while disregarding herself.

Third chakra healthy female

Developing, supporting, and receiving the fruits of his labors; assisting with his work efforts where possible; developing herself

Fourth chakra

Fourth chakra blocked female

In the victim role, she may engage in self-sacrificing martyr behaviors, such as provoking guilt in family members or manipulating them for attention.

In the abuser role, she may become dictatorial.

In the rescuer role, she may substitute duty and obligation for love.

Fourth chakra healthy female

Loving, compassionate, forgiving; offers emotional strength and direction

At this level, if her partner's heart chakra is not open, the woman may feel frustrated that her love is not received or acknowledged and that her partner does not understand her sensitive appreciation of love, ideals, and higher aspirations. She may look for this kind of connection inside of her own heart, becoming more interested in spirituality or religion in an effort to find solutions for her partnership situation. Because her energy level is higher, she may find comfort in meditation or fall in love with God. Otherwise, she will likely place her heart in total devotion to her family and tolerate her partner, sublimating her own feelings.

Fourth chakra blocked male

He may have difficulty receiving her love and remain stuck in his third chakra, where he avoids intimacy, sharing, and family connectedness. He may become addicted to work, with no time for sharing quality time, activities, or sacred space with his partner.

In the victim role, he avoids intimacy, isolates, and withdraws emotionally. He cannot share his joy; rather, he negates it, creating guilt. He may retreat into cynicism, disconnected from the family.

In the abuser role, he is a rule-oriented disciplinarian, regimented and highly demanding. All of these qualities are substituted for love.

In the rescuer role, he develops self-sacrificing martyr behaviors.

Fourth chakra healthy male

He receives love from his partner and is therefore able to activate his fifth chakra for clear, direct communication.

Fifth chakra

Fifth chakra blocked male

He will be unable to process his feelings and sentiments, and he will not be able to communicate his innermost thinking to his partner. This blockage prevents exploration of new ideas, directions, and planning with his partner and impairs more efficient teamwork. Because he cannot communicate clearly, big misunderstandings can result. His female counterpart will feel stymied, unable to take initiatives further, or she will shed whole brain understanding, further limiting the exchange of information. A blocked throat chakra in the male holds back creative problem-solving for the couple and may lead to serious mistakes in decision-making.

In the victim role, he is silent, unable to express himself.

In the abuser role, he may engage in verbal attacks, blaming and threatening others.

In the rescuer role, he plays therapist, pacifying his partner but not sharing himself authentically.

Fifth chakra healthy male

An open throat chakra allows for exploring new options, travel, adventure, and new careers. It brings a renewed interest in life, which can lead to easier passage into the next phase of life. The ability to communicate directly and clearly makes for healthy, creative brainstorming and honest discussions with his partner about changing needs as the couple moves through different life stages.

Fifth chakra blocked female

Blockage makes it harder for her to have a perspective for the future, to plan for a creative mid-life shift, or to change to a "world-centric" view. Because of this, the higher plan for her life may not activate. The woman who gets stuck at this level cannot perceive his needs or activate her own, so she cannot see the "bigger picture." This may lead to rigid thinking or crystallized belief patterns that limit the couple's future plans and possibilities.

In the victim role, the woman avoids her partner, is incapable of listening to or hearing him, or talks about herself incessantly.

In the abuser role, she is rigid, responds to him judgmentally, and provides no real feedback.

In the rescuer role, she plays the good therapist, listening to what he says but never feeling or responding authentically.

Fifth chakra healthy female

Listening from her heart

Sixth chakra

Sixth chakra blocked female

In the abuser role, the woman may substitute criticism or narrow-minded responses for objectivity.

In the victim role, she may become blind to intuitive insight and a visionary overview.

In the rescuer role, she may make it her duty to instruct him in how he should think and what he should do.

Sixth chakra healthy female

She can access her intuition, vision, and broader view understanding. The couple is able to discover new creative interests or a higher path of service to the world. They support one another in their spiritual and intellectual pursuits, or they simply come to a similar world-view or philosophical position that reflects a newfound acknowledgement and appreciation of each other's individuality. They can both truly communicate with clarity and wisdom: "I see you."

Sixth chakra blocked male

In the victim role, he may feel confused, helpless, or threatened. He may find that people are always telling him what to think and do.

In the abuser role, he may resist advice or feedback. He may be rigid, stubborn, and critical of his partner, telling her that she is unable to see the point or that her viewpoint is naïve or unhelpful.

In the rescuer role, he praises his partner's viewpoint, takes it on, and lives it for her. Because he lacks genuine critical assessment and decision-making skills of his own, however, her viewpoint becomes his viewpoint.

Sixth chakra healthy male

He accepts her intuition and vision. The couple functions at the level described for the sixth chakra healthy female: acknowledging and appreciating each other's individuality and supporting each other's spiritual and intellectual pursuits. Their relationship reflects this clarity and wisdom.

Seventh chakra

Seventh chakra blocked male

He cannot initiate, inspire, or set in motion a new wave of purpose on which the woman can build. This results in both partners being blocked in finding higher meaning.

Seventh chakra healthy male

Full of purpose and inspiration, able to initiate and implement new ideas more easily

Seventh chakra blocked female

In the victim role, she will follow him and take his orders, but she may be unable to receive any inspiration or implement new ideas on her own.

In the abuser role, she may act judgmental and feel like there is no higher purpose in life, assuming that his fanciful imagination and ideas have no merit.

In the rescuer role, she will take on as her responsibility whatever her partner establishes as his purpose.

Seventh chakra healthy female and male

At the level of the seventh chakra, the couple becomes one, united in divine androgyny, but their individual selves are also energetically complete. They might celebrate with this awareness: "To know you is to know myself."

Modern research and non-local healing

Before concluding this book with a number of exercises and meditations that you can do at home, either alone or with your partner, I'd like to introduce a concept that has profound implications for non-local healing and our efforts to achieve divine androgyny. As Ervin Laszlo discusses in *The Chaos Point* (2006, pp. 89–95), *holism*—the interconnectedness of all things in the world—is being verified by several branches of science including physics, biology, and psychology. Let's look at some of the research Laszlo explores and think about what it might mean for healing our relationships.

Holism in physics

The advent of quantum physics—the study of ultra-small domains of reality called *quanta,* which can be thought of as subatomic energy packets—opened the door to a better understanding of *non-locality,* a common behavior of quanta. As had been theorized by the renowned Austrian physicist Erwin Schrödinger in the 1930s and first physically measured by French physicist Alain Aspect in the 1980s, "the fundamental units of the physical world prove to be intrinsically and instantly 'entangled' with each other" (Laszlo, 2006, p. 90). When Aspect's experiment is carried out, a strange thing takes place: No matter how far two particles in the same state are separated, when the spin of one of them is measured, the spin of the other corresponds precisely to the measurement of the first. It is as if the second particle "knows" what is happening to the first. Aspect's findings have now been verified in laboratories in many areas of the world, at the atomic as well as the subatomic level, thus proving the most relevant (and strange) feature of the time- and space-transcending entanglement that physicists call non-locality:

> ...all quanta in the universe, most directly those that share or have ever shared the same quantum state, remain intrinsically connected with each other. This is both a microphysical and a cosmological phenomenon. It involves the very smallest as well as the very largest structures of the universe.
>
> Non-locality tells us that all things are interconnected and all are part of more integrated ensembles called *wholes*. (Laszlo, 2006, pp. 91–92)

Holism in psychology

Other modern research demonstrates what have come to be known as *telesomatic* effects—changes triggered in a targeted person's body by the mental processes of another. A variety of physiological effects have been shown to be transmissible in a nonsensory manner, and these in turn have implications for psychological processes. In the early 1970s, Laszlo writes, physicists Russell Targ and Harold Puthoff performed experiments on thought and image transference:

> They placed the "receiver" in a sealed, opaque, and electrically shielded chamber, and the "sender" in another room where he or she was subjected to bright flashes of light at regular intervals. The brain-wave patterns of both sender and receiver were registered on electroencephalograph (EEG) machines. As expected, the sender exhibited the rhythmic brain waves that normally accompany exposure to bright flashes of light. After a brief interval, however, the receiver also began to produce the same patterns, although the receiver was not being directly exposed to the flashes and was not receiving sense-perceivable signals from the sender.... (Laszlo, 2006, p. 94)

Laszlo notes that telesomatic effects recall the processes anthropologists refer to as "sympathetic magic," a practice widespread among traditional peoples. Often performed by shamans, witch doctors, and other practitioners who work on an effigy rather than directly on the person, sympathetic magic can result in dramatic physical effects, such as when a person whose effigy is being stabbed by a witch doctor falls ill, becomes lethargic, and even dies. Dean Radin and his University of Nevada collaborators studied a similar nonsensory transmission. They decided to test under controlled laboratory conditions what would happen if a positive variant of sympathetic magic was used. As Laszlo reports:

> In Radin's experiments, the subjects created a small doll in their own image and provided various objects (pictures, jewelry, an autobiography, and personally meaningful tokens) to "represent" them. They also gave a list of what makes them feel nurtured and comfortable. These and the accompanying information were used by the "healers" (who functioned analogously to the "senders" in thought- and image-transfer experiments) to create a sympathetic connection to the subjects (the "patients"). The patients were wired up to monitor the activity of their autonomous nervous system—electrodermal activity, heart rate, blood pulse volume. The healers were in an acoustically and electromagnetically shielded room in an adjacent building. The healers placed the doll and other small objects on the table in front of them and concentrated on them while sending randomly sequenced "nurturing" (active healing) and "rest" messages.
>
> It turned out that the electrodermal activity and heart rates of the patients were significantly different during the active nurturing periods than during the rest periods, and blood pulse volume was significant for a few seconds during the nurturing periods. Both heart rate and blood flow indicated a "relaxation response," which makes sense because the healer was attempting to "nurture" the subject via the doll. On the other hand, a higher rate of electrodermal activity showed that the patient's autonomic

nervous system was becoming aroused. Why this should be so was puzzling until the experimenters realized that the healers nurtured the patients by rubbing the shoulders of the dolls that represented them, or stroking the doll's hair and face. This, apparently, had the effect of a "remote massage" on the patients…. Radin and his colleagues concluded that the actions and intentions of the healer are mimicked in the patient almost as if they were next to each other. (Laszlo, 2006, pp. 95–96)

The researchers found that the distance between the sender and receiver made little difference in the outcome. The parapsychologists William Braud and Marilyn Schlitz confirmed this effect in a large number of experiments:

…They found that the mental images of the sender could "reach out over space" to cause changes in the distant receiver. The effects are comparable to those that one's own mental processes produce on one's body. "Telesomatic" action by a distant person is nearly as effective as "psychosomatic" action by the subject on himself or herself. (Laszlo, p. 96)

Laszlo further elaborates on the research into telesomatic effects in his exceptional later work, *Quantum Shift in the Global Brain:*

Additional evidence of the transmission of physical effect between individuals in the absence of sensory contact is furnished by spiritual healing. Psychiatrist Daniel Benor analyzed hundreds of cases of controlled experiments in spiritual and nonlocal healing and found significant evidence of positive therapeutic effect.

The transfer of effect from healer to patient can be monitored and measured: it shows up in their EEG waves. C. Maxwell Cade of the Institute of Electrical Engineers in England tested the EEG patterns of over 3,000 people in various states of consciousness. He found five characteristic states, where each state manifests a specific combination of wave frequencies (the known frequencies are beta, with a range between 13 and 30 Hz; alpha, ranging from 8 to 13

Hz; theta, between 4 and 7 Hz; and delta, in the range of 0.5 to 4 Hz). The normal waking state is almost entirely in the range of beta. Alpha occurs in meditation and restful states, theta in half-awake or dreaming-sleep states, and delta in profound dreamless sleep. Healers function typically in what Cade called the "fifth" state, consisting of a moderate amount of beta and theta, wide alpha, and no delta…. Cade found that in the process of healing the healer induces his or her characteristic fifth state pattern in the patient. (Laszlo, 2008, p. 107)

Clearly, the discoveries of modern researchers mentioned above, as well as ongoing explorations into the nature of human consciousness, have profound implications for helping us heal our personal relationships and our planet as a whole.

Divine Androgyny: Exercises and Meditations

Meditation for healing and connecting your male and female aspects

Close your eyes and breathe deeply. Relax your body. As you breathe, place your attention on your feet. Feel the healing golden light flowing through your feet, up into your legs. Feel the healing light as it flows up to your thighs, hips, pelvic area, and abdomen. Feel the healing light as it moves to your chest, your heart, your shoulders, and down through your arms and into your hands and fingers, just relaxing you. The healing light is flowing to your neck, your head, your face. And, now, begin to visualize a golden ball of light above your head. And let go of all your worries and concerns, just letting them go into that golden ball of light. Let that light go out into the great universe. And ask that the universe take these thoughts and place them in harmony and order, that they will return to you when you need them in perfect harmony and order.

Now, as you breathe, imagine a warm pink cloud is spreading beneath you, lifting you up, and taking you to the ocean side. See yourself there on the beach connecting with the sun, the wind, the water. Find a comfortable place to lie down on the beach. You look up to the sky above you, a beautiful clear blue sky. No clouds in the sky, just a golden sun, the source of your healing power. Feel the golden sun now as a ray of light coming into your heart, connecting you with the source of healing power. Feel yourself lifting into the light...higher and freer, lighter and higher, and freer and lighter and higher. Lifting, lifting, all the way up into a beautiful garden of healing light.

Now, feel yourself stepping into the garden, receiving its harmony and love and peace. For you are harmony, love and peace, true in yourself. When you are ready, step out of this garden of harmony, love and peace and feel yourself again lifting into the light, higher than before—higher and freer, lighter and higher, freer and higher and lighter, freer and higher and lighter and freer—up to the golden sun, your source of healing power. As you reach the golden sun, say a prayer within your heart for your healing. Open your crown chakra to receive all the sun's healing light, through the top of your head and all the way down into your body. Heart, arms, legs, hands, feet. And when you are ready, step back into this golden ray of healing light and gradually come down in the shaft of this ray of light. Find your way to your physical body and awareness. Take a deep breath to signal to yourself that you are back. Keeping your eyes closed, remain in this relaxed energy, beginning to focus on the center of your heart.

Now, as you focus on your heart, imagine yourself walking into a garden. Call on your male and female energies to appear with you in the garden. Look at them now. What emotions, actions or behaviors do they express? What negative emotions or behaviors do you feel or see in them? Ask yourself which of the energies, male or female, appears to be most wounded and in need of healing. Talk to this aspect of yourself, and let it describe to you what wounding or negative elementals it is holding for someone in your life, a parent or a caretaker. As you identify who these negative energies belong to, bring them into the garden. And give back to them these energies that are not yours. As you give them back, be clear with that parent or caretaker what you are giving back to them. And now, take a sword of light in your hand and, on the count of three, cut that connection with them. One, two, three...cut. And breathe deeply. Breathe in the new healing light in your heart center. Let the Christ or your parent or caretaker's guardian angel take them into the light for healing.

Now focus your attention on the other aspect of yourself, the male or female aspect that has been watching you give back the energies held by its counterpart, healing that aspect of you. What negative emotions or behavior is this aspect carrying? Who are they holding it for? As you ask these questions, let the light of the Christ, or spiritual guide of your choosing, reach through the first aspect that was healed, touching the second aspect with golden light. Let the shining golden light transform whatever decisions or beliefs or negative energies the second aspect is holding. Feel the spiritual energy flowing through the first aspect. Turn again to the second aspect and feel again what limiting energies it is carrying. Now, call on the person, the caretaker, the parent that gave you this wounding. And give back to that parent or caretaker whatever you are holding for them. Take a sword of light in your hand and, at the count of three, cut the connecting cord as you give back these energies. One, two, three…cut. Breathing deeply, ask for the help of the light and send that parent into the light for healing.

Now, let the spiritual light flow into the second aspect of yourself. And feel the heart healed by the golden healing light, as the old feelings and beliefs dissolve. Let the golden light transform all the negative energies. And allow your healed male and female aspects to stand before each other. Let them embrace each other with love. Feel the Christ, or spiritual guide of your choosing, connecting them as he threads a golden thread of light from the male's first chakra to the female's first chakra. And feel the female bringing this golden thread of light to her second chakra, sending it to the male's second chakra. Feel him receiving this energy in his second chakra and drawing it up to his third chakra. And now he sends the golden thread of light to her third chakra, and she receives this golden thread of light in her third chakra, drawing this energy up into her fourth chakra. Let her send this energy now to his fourth chakra, and feel him receiving the energy in his fourth chakra, drawing it up into his fifth chakra, and sending it back to her fifth chakra. And now the energy is moving to her sixth chakra, and back to his sixth chakra. Feel the energy growing as the male aspect takes the energy into his sixth chakra and draws it into his seventh chakra. And now he sends this divine golden thread of energy to her seventh chakra, completing the circle of light and love between them. Take a few moments to feel their deep love for each other, their respect for each other. And you feel them coming together as one, as you bring them into your heart. And when you are ready, return from your meditation to physical awareness.

Meditation for experiencing your four bodies and the universal body of God

Close your eyes and, as you breathe, relax. Just take in a warm and cleansing breath. Begin to feel your body, your feet. Feel your legs, your torso, arms, and head. And bring your attention to your breathing, the rise and fall of your breath. With every breath, life-giving oxygen enters your blood. This oxygen is charged with your etheric prana or energy. The prana charges your energy body...it charges your physical body. Feel yourself in your body, breathing this life-giving prana. Feel yourself in your body, receiving the life-giving prana, your etheric vitality. And notice how this energy comes not only through your lungs and through the air, but it is entering through the energy centers, the chakras in your body. It comes in through the center of the bottom of your feet, through the center below your navel and above your pubic bone, the chi center, and through your heart chakra, through the palms of your hands and through your crown chakra. And within your physical body, many small chakras are opening up to receive this etheric vitality. On your fingertips, the swirls, the imprints on your palms, these chakras are receiving the etheric vitality that the holy archangels are giving to your physical body.

Feel the movement in your blood. And the holy archangels—Michael, Raphael, and Gabriel—are working in your blood. The flow of your blood feeds all the cells in your body, exchanging and releasing all the impurities. The iron in your blood vibrates with the core of the earth, the domain of archangel Michael. Feel archangel Michael on the right side of your physical body in red flames of light, Raphael on the left in violet flames of light, and Gabriel behind you in sky-blue flames of light. Together, they are maintaining your physical body. Fire, air, and water combining with the matter of your body. You are a living being within your physical body. Give thanks for this, for all the work the archangels are doing for you. As you breathe and feel the work of Michael, Raphael, and Gabriel in your physical body, feel your etheric vitality growing. As you feel yourself within your physical body, know that you have a physical body, but you are not the physical body.

Now, feel the Christ, or spiritual guide of your choosing, coming to you and gently reaching in, taking the hands of your emotional body, and lifting you gently out of your physical body. Feel yourself in your emotional body, your astral body. Feel the qualities and nature of your astral body. Raphael and Gabriel work primarily in your astral body. Feel Raphael on your left and Gabriel on your right. Feel their blessings, and feel the qualities that they bring to your astral body. In this body, you can be in more than one place at a time, and through the law of attunement you can be in this fourth dimensional energy with other souls. Feel yourself in your astral body. Feel the love of Gabriel, the clarity of Raphael feeding this body. From your emotional, astral body, you can know the inner feelings and sentiments of all living beings on earth and within the other dimensions. And from this body you can communicate most directly with the children of the earth, children up to around seven years of age. Everything for them is magic, the wonder of life. The astral body connects you to this magic, and you can meet the children you know on earth here in your astral body. Acknowledge them now and see in their little eyes how they react to seeing you here. You can also contact the inner child here, because most of the childhood memories of adults live in the astral body. Now, look at someone in your life that you love, perhaps your partner or some other adult. Contact them now through your astral body. What do you experience? Do they respond to you? The Christ once said: "Unless you are like little children, you cannot enter the kingdom of the heaven." For the astral kingdom is the first heaven. Feel yourself in your astral body. From this body you can contact the souls of your beloved ones who have departed. You can contact a grandparent, a parent, or anyone else you loved who has left the physical world. Through your thoughts and feelings, feel them coming to you as you call them. Send them your love and feel them returning their love to you. Your loved ones are not gone. They are here within this astral dimension with you. Communicate whatever you need to say to them that was never said before, that they never heard. In your astral body, you can contact the world on the astral level, with the great sentiments and feelings and light, with the life that goes on after we all leave the physical body. You are in your astral body, made of vibrant light; your cells are light. On the astral plane, you don't need a light, a candle, a lamp to guide your way. You are the source of your light. And you are in your astral body, but you are not your astral body.

Feel your spiritual guide appearing again. Very gently he reaches inside of you, taking the hands of your mental body, a body of a more expanded light. Feel yourself being lifted out of your astral body by your spiritual guide and into your mental body, and now feel yourself in your mental body. Here the work of Raphael and Michael is the greatest. Feel Raphael on your left and Michael on your right. In your mental body, you are connected with the past, the present and the future of time. In this body, you can know all your lives and all the recorded and unrecorded history of the past. In your mental body, thoughts are reality, for when you say "I am," you become what you focus on. When the Christ said "I am the light of the world," he was speaking from the soul through the mental body of all humanity. For in the mental body, you can be connected to all things, all universes, at once. Feel Raphael and Michael working on your mental body. Here in the mental body, you become a planetary and universal being, the body of the higher mind of God. Here you receive the teachings of wisdom and love from all the great masters and prophets throughout time. Here in the mental body, you create the future conditions of your life and of the world. And here you can understand why you chose your incarnation as you have and the meaning of it. Contact the teachers of the centuries, the ascended masters, through your mental body. Feel yourself also contacting the souls of other universes, for you can travel everywhere in your mental body. In your mental body, you can contact the archetypes, the pure archetypes of male and female, Adam and Eve. You can know their thoughts and their feelings, what they experienced through physical incarnation, and you can know all the languages that have existed through time. Feel yourself in your mental body. This is the home of your permanent personality, the part of your individuality that goes on eternally, life after life, gaining experience, guiding and assisting your temporal personality. Give thanks for your mental body and for the work of Michael and Raphael. You are in your mental body, but you are not your mental body.

Feel your spiritual guide coming to you again, this time reaching into your heart and taking the hands of your soul. Feel the brilliant light of your soul, its infinite love and joy. Feel your spiritual guide taking your soul in his hands, and feel yourself lifting and expanding into a spiraling column of light. Every time you spiral wider, your soul expands more and more. Freer and higher, lighter and freer, freer and lighter, lighter and higher and freer. As your soul rises higher, feel yourself approaching the enormous golden light of God, the great ocean of love and mercy. For even though you are intensely bright and much larger than you have ever imagined, you are simply one atom in the infinite body of God. Feel yourself merging into the universal body of God. And yet you are still an individual. Feel yourself now as the soul you really are. "I am that I am. I am that I am."

Now, feel your spiritual guide gently taking the hands of your soul. And as you step out of the universal body of God, know that you will never leave this absolute infinite beingness, for you are always within this beingness, even now. For all your lower bodies are the projected light of your soul into the worlds of matter, the worlds of earth. As your spiritual guide walks with you over a beautiful landscape of flowers and plants and trees, the land of the soul, feel the one great quality that exists there beyond all others—the quality of divine love and charity. As Saint Paul said to the Corinthians, "If I have faith, hope and charity, of these three charity is the greatest, for this is the true nature of the soul." For the soul is divine love in its expression through the worlds, through all the bodies. Now feel your spiritual guide leading your soul back into your mental body, and feel your soul entering your mental body. Even though your mental body possesses great powers, the soul has shown it that all that really matters is love. Let your soul's light of love fill your mental body and transform it. And let this light of the soul reflect through all the universes, communicating to your mental body the one great truth: The soul exists because of God's love for the soul. And the soul is the light and sound of God. Whatever you experience in your mental body, if it comes from the soul, it is filled with charity, kindness, love and tolerance. Feel these qualities of the soul coming through your mental body for all of life.

Feel your spiritual guide before you again. This time, feel your spiritual guide taking you back into your emotional, your astral, body connecting you to this body again. Feel your soul in your astral body. Love is what your soul brings to the astral body, and many great qualities—harmony and peace, patience, wisdom and love. Feel these qualities growing within your astral body as they flow in from your soul. You are the soul within your astral body. Can you feel your connection to other souls on the astral plane? What can you communicate from your soul to the others through your astral body? Can you see the beauty in everyone? The feeling of oneness? The enthusiasm and inspiration? The joy of feeling? The laughter?

Feel your spiritual guide appearing once again before you, this time taking your hand and leading your soul with your mental and astral bodies into your physical body. Feel your soul within your physical body and awareness. Feel your soul's light filling all your cells, your tissues, your organs, your brain and nervous system, your blood, your bones, your senses. How do you experience your senses from the soul's perspective in your physical body? Your hearing, your sight, your touch, your taste, your smell? What do you understand now about being in a physical body that you did not understand before? Feel your soul within your physical body. And let the light of your soul and its love activate the DNA within your body that is waiting to be awakened to new abilities, to new consciousness, to your life as Homo spiritus now. Now. Now.

Now feel your spiritual guide as he stands before you with a smile and the radiant eyes of love. Feel his love entering your heart, your physical human heart. Feel him holding in his hands a beautiful pink rose. Hear him saying, "My beloved, take this mystic rose that I give to you. Place it within your human heart to protect your soul in your body. And allow the soul to experience life in a new way. See everything now through divine love." Feel your spiritual guide holding a beautiful cup filled with etheric vitality. Drink up this cup of etheric vitality, for it is the drink to quench the thirst that no water can extinguish. And feel yourself again in your physical body and awareness. Begin to move your body, stretching. Rub your hands together, faster and faster. Massage your face. And awaken.

Using different colors to energetically help yourself, your partner, and your children by building and sending positive elementals

As Daskalos taught, you can use different colors for healing yourself or others. You can send these healing energies to your loved ones, to people who are requesting healing from you, and also directly to yourself. You can use these colors to build positive elementals to place in your surroundings or send out into the world. You can also program a color elemental to come to you when you most need its particular healing energy. It is important to remember that you should never send energy to anyone for a specific purpose unless you have that person's permission. Doing so would be interfering in that person's life, and it would really tie you up with his or her karma. Keep this in mind when you work with sending energy. If you want to send healing energy for the world in general, or for your community or country, that is okay. You can send general-purpose energy for a person's highest good as long as you don't send it according to your own agenda or without that person having requested or being open to it.

The following meditation helps you feel and heal with three colors— rose pink, sky blue, and canary yellow—and white. Once you learn this meditation, you can use it with other colors as well. (A color chart follows the meditation.)

With your eyes closed, bring your palms together and feel the energy between them. And feel the border of the energy as you create a ball of white light in the palms of your hands. Now, feel the energy of the ball and breathe more energy into it, strengthening it. And with your intention, with your thoughts building energy and moving energy, place a picture or image of yourself into this white ball of light. How does it feel to hold a white ball of light? Feel how your feelings are changing.

Now, allow yourself to change the color of the ball of light, visualizing and changing the light to a rose-pink ball of light. If you have trouble seeing the light changing color, just say to the light, "You are a rose-pink ball of light that I am holding." How does it feel to hold a rose-pink ball of light? What is its vibration? What are the qualities of this rose-pink light compared to the white light? How do you feel now?

Take a deep breath and let go of the rose-pink color. As you breathe, create a beautiful sky-blue ball of light. What does it feel like to hold a blue ball of light? How is it different from the white or the rose-pink ball of light?

And, now, breathing deeply again, let the blue color go and create a bright canary yellow ball. How does it feel to hold a yellow ball of light? How is it different from the white, rose-pink, and blue balls of light?

One last time, let this yellow color go and create a white ball of light again. Feel the white light that you are holding in your hands. As you hold this ball of white light, imagine placing an image of yourself in the light and say, "I send you love and good will and God's blessings." As you say these words, you are imprinting love and good will and God's blessings. And now, holding the white ball of light in your hands, very gently bring the ball into your physical chest, your heart. Breathe it in now and feel the white light spreading throughout your body, bringing you the message that you have imprinted into it. And, gently now, just disconnect and open your eyes.

For general healing and to bring more harmony into your shared space in partnership, these three colors work very well. You can also send the colors into specific chakras. In the meditation, we drew white light into the heart chakra for dispersal to the rest of the body. When we send blue to the solar plexus, we send the energy of peace and harmony. When we send rose pink to the heart, we send the energy of love, compassion, and forgiveness. We can send yellow to the head center for mental clarity and understanding. We send white to the top of the head to activate spiritual purpose and soul connection, and we can also use white for general distance healing when someone hasn't expressed any particular problem but is "happy to receive energy."

White contains all the colors. Daskalos often said that if you don't know what color of light to send, then send white light and the archangels will take from the white the color vibration that is needed to heal the person. So if you are ever uncertain about what color to work with for yourself or others, use white. Just send white to the heart of the recipient and the archangels will send whatever is needed.

The following chart shows other colors and how they are used in healing. You can substitute any of these colors for the ones used in the meditation if you want to work on a specific problem area. If you are

Non-local Color Healing

Color	Chakra	To Treat	To Create
Red	4th, Heart	Fatigue Anemia Low blood pressure	Love Energy
Rose pink	4th, Heart	Wounded self-esteem Emotional disappointment Anger	Self-esteem Self-value
Bright orange	5th, Throat	Seriousness Hormonal imbalances Viral illnesses Blood disorders	Joy Laughter Happiness Increased immunity
Canary yellow	6th, Brow	Mental confusion Mental fatigue Lack of focus Scattered thoughts	Mental focus Intellectual clarity Concentration
Emerald green	3rd, Solar plexus	Physical pain Inflammation, infection Arthritis Allergies Autoimmune conditions Broken bones Emotional frustration, stress	Peace Harmony
Turquoise	6th, Brow	Anxiety	Faith Trust
Sky blue	3rd, Solar plexus	Violent, strong emotions Anger Hatred Resentment	Peace Harmony
Indigo	6th, Brow	Obsessive-compulsive thinking Tormenting thoughts Self-criticism Arrogance Pride	Ego balancing Humility
Violet	6th, Brow	Decision-making Mental confusion Negative beliefs	Mental clarity and focus Concentration Connecting with higher wisdom and thinking
White	4th, Heart	All conditions	Healing and improvement

sending to another person, it is good for them to know when you are doing it. You can ask them to be quiet at that time, even lie down or sit down, and close their eyes. This way, they will be more open to receiving the healing energies. You can do the same thing for yourself, if needed. You visualize yourself in the ball of light and ask for the highest healing possible for the situation. You can imagine your illness being healed. You can visualize yourself being healthy and feeling good.

Here is a basic menu, or protocol, you can use:

1. If someone gives you a clear condition or problem and you know what color is needed, then send that color.

2. Emerald green is used mostly for inflammations and physical conditions. For emotional problems, blue is good. For mental problems, yellow can help.

3. If someone has chronic fatigue, then red light is what is needed. Red is very strong life energy, and they need more life-force, more yang energy.

4. Any time you are having a feeling of imbalance, just visualize white and the archangels will pull out the adequate color to correct the situation.

Unblocking and healing patterns of wounding in partnership

This exercise is intended to help you unblock and heal old wound patterns that prevent the natural flow and exchange of energy in your partnership. This exercise is optimally done together but can also be done alone with your partner's consent. You can repeat this exercise as often as you like.

1. Review the seven chakra energy exchange diagrams and decide together which chakra exchange is the most problematic for you. Work on that one first. At any time in the following exercise, you can refer back to these diagrams as needed.

2. Find a quiet, peaceful place where you can face each other sitting down. You may choose to put on relaxing music in the background.

3. You can begin by facing each other, holding hands, connecting your heart energies by visualizing energy flowing between your hearts in a figure eight, like an infinity symbol (∞). Or you can simply say a prayer that is meaningful to both of you or sing the mantra Hu for a few minutes with your eyes closed.

4. Share with each other, in a non-judgmental way, how the unhealthy or blocked exchange makes each of you feel. Caution: Do not attack the self-value of your partner. Avoid saying what the other "should" or "should not" do. Simply own your own feelings and share them with your partner.

5. Now, each of you close your eyes and imagine these feelings as a negative elemental, a collection of energy with a life of its own that exists between you. Take turns describing how this negative elemental looks and feels, its shape and colors, and anything else about the elemental that you imagine. You and your partner will likely have a different take on it, so together explore the way your elemental looks to you until you create a composite image or picture based on each of your contributions.

6. With your eyes still closed, and if you haven't already done so, visualize a set of eyes on the elemental. Look into its eyes.

7. You can now imagine dialoguing with this composite image, taking turns asking the elemental what it wants from each of you. Some questions you might ask could include, "How are you deceiving us, causing us to blame each other and distance ourselves from each other?" "What are you doing to cause our suffering?" "How are you causing us pain and disappointment?"

8. Take turns reflecting on what or who in your families of origin the thoughts and feelings connected to this elemental remind you of, and show those family members the pain that carrying these energies has caused you. Sense where each of you feels connected to the originator's negative energy—which chakra or area of the body feels tense or uncomfortable—and cut any unhealthy threads or cords of energy in these areas that are binding you. Release your family members to the divine light for healing and peace, forgiving them for what they have done or expected of you.

9. Now, again taking turns, ask yourself, "Based on what I took on and carried for my family members, what codependent role did I identify with? Victim? Abuser? Rescuer? And what role have I played out with my partner?" Tell the roles you took on, the elementals, that they are no longer needed in your partnership. Invite in a higher spiritual power: divine light, Christ love, or Archangel Michael's light of transformation. Ask the negative energies between you and your partner to be lifted up into the spiritual light.

10. Visualize flames of this transforming light dissolving the old energy. In its place, visualize a golden ball of light. Together, taking turns, create a positive elemental with the qualities or virtues suggested for the chakra you are working on. Feel and see the virtues flowing down a column of golden light, and accept and affirm the positive elemental. Feel the emotions and visualize new ways that you can both share in the benefits of this new elemental's positive energies.

11. Finally, take the golden ball of light into yourselves. If you like, you may complete this exercise by together lacing a golden thread of light through each of your seven chakra points, starting with the man's first chakra, as shown in the diagram of male–female dynamic exchange.

Nine-day ritual to manifest positive change

Background

This is an old Judeo-Christian ritual. It can be used to build powerful angelic elementals for protection of yourself, others, or your house.

Materials needed

1. White unscented candle, good quality
2. A high-vibration holy oil; frankincense or sandalwood is good
3. Rock incense in the same scents as the holy oil
4. Charcoal burners
5. Matches
6. An opening and closing prayer; can be traditional or whatever feels good to you.
7. A request and/or picture of someone

Summary of Process

1. Dip a finger in oil.
2. Do seven crosses on the candle with oil.
3. Light candle and incense (use charcoal burners)
4. Say a special prayer. You can use the Lord's Prayer or the Prayer to Mary/Maria Sophia
5. Read the request with love and reverence, reading it slowly and intently.
6. In silence, hold the situation or see the person in a ball of light for several minutes.
7. Say a closing prayer.
8. Put out the candle with a candle snifter; don't blow it out.

Notes

1. Start after nightfall, the same time each day, for nine days.
2. Start any day but Sunday, because Sunday is the day of rest.

3. The ritual is most powerful if you start it on a new or full moon.
4. It is best to get a picture of the person.
5. Sample requests: For physical ailments, lack of control with something, new home, relationship problems, smooth transitions, financial matters, self-healing, partnership issues, children.

The nine-day ritual is a very effective way to cleanse blocked energies and bring about new healing or a renewal of energy. This process involves requesting spiritual help to build a good positive energy to assist in healing yourself, your children, your family, your partnerships, or whatever else you wish to heal.

The list of materials needed and the overall process are summarized above. It is important that the healing request is written clearly and precisely on a piece of paper, but the request should not be demanding or controlling. Write it from your heart, and ask for the highest result. If you are doing this for your children or for yourself and your relationship, you can make the request in many ways. For example, in the case of your children, you can have a picture of them on the table so that you are looking at them and connecting with them while making your request.

On the first night of the ritual, place an unlit candle and charcoal burner with rock incense on the table. Dip your finger into the holy oil, then in arbitrary places through the whole candle draw seven crosses. Light the candle and the rock incense, and wait a moment until they are burning and smoking. Hold the piece of paper with your prayer and request in front of you. Say the beginning prayer, and then very lovingly read your request. You can do this silently or aloud, reading slowly and with intention. You can address the request to the Holy Spirit, to the Divine Mother or Father, to the Christ or the archangels or any of your spiritual helpers. After reading your request, you may remain silent for a few minutes. You can also hold a ball of light between the palms of your hands and hold a loving image of your child or partner or whoever you are making the healing request for. Or you can hold their picture in your hands and see it filled with light. Then say a closing prayer. Finally, snuff the candle out. For best results, do this ritual for nine consecutive nights, normally after dark. Try to do it at around the same time each day. Don't begin it on a Sunday, which is considered a day of rest, but you can begin on any other day. Once you have started, continue through Sunday to reach the nine nights. On the last night, let the candle burn completely down instead of snuffing it out. (Of course, make sure the candle is burning in a place where nothing will catch on fire.)

So, why nine days? Nine is the number of completion and wholeness. Performing the ritual at the same physical location is best, but if you happen to be travelling you can also do it wherever you are. Do it when you can do it quietly, without disturbance, when the kids are already in bed, no cats and dogs are coming in demanding food or attention, and any distracting electronics are turned off. Each night, in this quiet place, you will build more and more positive energy during this process. What you are actually doing over the nine days of the ritual is building a very powerful, positive elemental, and you are also pushing negative elementals out of your energy field. The positive elemental is similar to a guardian angel or protector, so after the nine days you may feel much more peaceful and safe.

It can happen sometimes that you will feel discomfort for the first few days. This is because the negative elementals are fighting against being pushed out by the positive elemental you are creating. Maybe they will try to keep you from doing the ritual by saying things like, "I ate too much tonight; I am tired; I can wait until tomorrow; there is a special TV program on tonight." So you have to discipline yourself to do the ritual and to keep the process going to build the energy. Sometimes after you have done this nine-day process, you experience immediate results. There is a real shift in the energy. At other times, nothing will seem to be happening at first. Suddenly, though, situations may arise that challenge you in some way to learn something. And once those spiritual lessons are learned, the original situation that you wanted to change begins to shift, and what you wanted to happen finds its way into being. So be aware of this. Don't despair if something doesn't happen immediately. Your prayers are heard, and the energy is created, but sometimes it takes time to make things happen.

The other thing to be aware of is that you can repeat the nine-day ritual, but I recommend waiting at least a month or two to do this. You can do it first for yourself, for your own healing and for your own path, then do it for your partnership, and then do it for your children. If you feel like you are already undergoing enough healing within yourself, then start with the partnership and then go on to the children. If you feel like everything is okay in your partnership, just do the healing ritual with your children. There is a spiritual law called the law of efficiency, which means that when your energy is really aligned and focused on something, then you open as a clear channel for this change to take place. But if you are scattered in your request, your results may be less focused. It is better to perform the ritual once with focus and attention than to do it several times in an inattentive way. Also, a nice thing about this ritual is that it is a very nice meditation practice. When you are doing it, it is a really special time when you feel cleansed. Most people start sleeping better. The vibrations of the incense and candle cleanse the house. It is better, however, not to do this ritual in your bedroom unless you can air it out completely before you go to sleep.

During the process of doing the nine-day ritual, it can happen that you feel like adding something to your request, something to improve it or correct something about the request. What is happening is that, as you pay more attention to the request, the Holy Spirit brings more clarity to you about your request. You can make these corrections or additions that occur to you, but it is better to make any changes within the first few days. You can make any kind of request: involving physical illnesses, lack of control in life, your new home or flat, relationship issues, financial matters, the New Year, whatever. For yourself, you can ask what is in the highest good for your soul's evolution in the area of the issue you request for. You can also ask more generally for help and change if something has been bothering you for a very long time. The help you need will come.

Advanced practice for letting go of criticism, fear, and pride

You can do the following three practices with a partner. These are very strong exercises that can help you liberate yourself from the codependency elementals of criticism, fear, or pride so you can let go of any related thoughts, feelings, or actions that may have enslaved you.

Exercise for criticism: Abuser role

1. Close your eyes and allow yourself to think of someone that you are having difficulties with, someone that you have criticized. Bring this person before you. Share with them what upsets you about them, what you feel you have to criticize in them. As you do this, become aware of all of your thoughts, feelings, and body sensations.

2. Now, take a deep breath. Imagine yourself stepping out of your body, your mind, your heart and stepping into their body, mind, and heart. How does it feel to be judged by you? What is this person that you have criticized experiencing?

3. Step in a little deeper into their heart and soul, the heart of love. Feel this heart of love and the love inside of them, their capacity for love.

4. Now, step out of their mind, their body, their heart and come back into your own body, mind and heart. Look into their eyes. What do you feel and see now? How did this experience change your thoughts and feelings about them?

5. Let divine love join you, touching your heart, becoming your loving self. Look at the other person again. What do you experience now? Can you forgive them? Can you connect with their source of love that is your source of love, the truth of love beyond your personalities?

6. Speak from your heart to them, and allow them to respond to you from their heart. What do you experience now? Take a deep breath…and gradually open your eyes when you are ready.

It may take time to shift your view. If the elemental that is "the critical one" tries to stay between you, it will warp your perception. If, after doing this exercise a number of times, the critical self persists, then you'll have to deal directly with the critical self. The mirror technique is useful for this purpose. You just look into the mirror, looking into the eyes of your critical self, and feel it judging and criticizing you. Really look, really see, this critical one and say, "I am not you. You are not me. I created you to protect something inside of me. I don't need your protection any more. I have created you to protect my inner child, and I need to let you go." Tell the critical self how much it hurts you, and how it hurts the people that you love. Really use your imagination to break away from this critical self. Take your sword of light and cut the energy cords that bind you to it, or imagine the archangels taking it into the light. Or send the critical self off on a nice vacation, to a place where it can relax and recharge.

If you want to send the critical one to, say, Siberia, then the critical elemental is very alive in you; it is functioning like a trickster, creating more critics so it can keep criticizing even when you think you have sent it away. So send your critical self to a nice place, and be loving with it. Then call on the spirit of compassion to fill you with light and new vision. The spirit of compassion represents tolerance, acceptance, and neutrality and always takes the middle way. When the critical one is off on vacation, repeat the exercise for criticism again with the other person.

Exercise for fear: Victim role

You need a partner. (If you have a friend or counselor to be the mediator for this exercise, it may free you up to go deeper and allow you to feel more safety.) You stand and face each other. The amount of transformation you get from this exercise depends on the amount of commitment and focus you put into it, so don't be inhibited. One of you will take the role of the Christ self, or spiritual guide of your choosing, which means that you just hold the space with unconditional love. The person in the role of the spiritual self serves as a figure of trust and safety for the other and holds a neutral, loving space for the partner who will be going into a place of fear. The one going into the fear will recall a situation of being very afraid and, following the steps below, will connect with that feeling. The important thing for this partner is just to go into the fear instead of avoiding feeling. After doing the exercise, the partners can reverse roles and do it again. Those who don't have a lot of fear to release may not respond as deeply to the exercise.

So, when you are ready to begin the exercise, face each other and decide who will be the spiritual energy and who will go into a fearful situation. Now, both of you close your eyes for a moment. Breathe deeply. If you are the partner playing the spiritual self, focus on your heart and silently repeat a mantra that helps you hold a safe, loving space: "I am Divine Love" or "Christ have mercy on us" or "Hu." Hold the energy in your heart and hold the space open for love. If you wish, you can imagine the Christ, or spiritual guide of your choosing, coming up to you and connecting with you, saying, "I am your light. I am your love. I am the source." Hold this energy.

The partner who is going into fear follows these instructions: Allow yourself to remember moments of fear in life, a time when fear was in your eyes. Let your body, mind, and soul stay in complete fear. Go deeper and deeper into the fear. Deeper and deeper. You are alone. Allow your body to begin to express the fear by taking a position—maybe crouching or cowering or whatever position your body takes in response to feeling the fear—and allow the fear to become more vivid to you. You are terrified. Feel this fear coming out of your second chakra. Your whole body wants to express it. Feel the fear growing stronger and stronger until, when you are totally inside this energy of your fear, let yourself express it. Give voice to your fear. Listen to your fear. What does it sound like? Feel your fear deeply. What does its voice want to say? What do you want to say?

When the fear begins to be verbalized, if you are the one playing the spiritual self, open your eyes. If you are the one experiencing the fear, stay with it. Let yourself go deeper. When you were afraid, what did you want to say? What did you want the world to hear? Say it aloud to your partner. Say it again. Open your eyes and look into the eyes of your spiritual guide. The one playing the spiritual self is now showering you with love and green light. Open yourself to receive the love and understanding that comes from this divine presence before you. Imagine a door between you and the spiritual self; it is up to you to trust and have the courage to step through that door into the arms of divine love. When you are ready, reach out and embrace the spiritual self, feeling this divine loving energy, safety and trust. Feel the love and peace spreading through you. Thank your partner for supporting you, for being there for you. Now, take a deep breath and shake out your body. Then change roles and do the exercise again.

Exercise for pride: Rescuer role
You can do this one alone. Take several deep, cleansing breaths and

relax your body. Feel the healing white light flowing up from your feet into your body. Visualize yourself walking into a garden. As you walk about, bring into the garden all of the people in your life that you've felt like you had to rescue. Begin to speak out loud, saying, "I know better! I am better than they are! What would they do without me?" Now speak to them: "Look what I've done for you. If you didn't have me, where would you be? You all depend on me!" Walk about, really showing them your pride, and think to yourself, "Oh, how needy and helpless they are. But I am so responsible, so caring." Intensify your feeling of pride by saying to yourself, "You're the greatest. No one is better than you are. You are the only one who knows or cares about anything."

Magnify your pride and then shout at the others: "I am indispensable to you! You give nothing worth my while in return. You'd probably die without me!" Stop, breathe deeply, and exhale slowly. Look at yourself; see how proud you are, how great you are, how wonderful you are. You are the only one, the best! Holding this prideful awareness, allow yourself to see your life passing by from this high position, above everybody else.

Now, look into the eyes of all those you've taken care of and ask yourself what you are expecting in return. How have you blinded yourself to the contributions they've attempted to give to you? You see that some of them are angry or sad, or even as proud as you are, but you see that at least one of them really loves you and has served you as well as possible. Allow this person's love to be like a flashlight lighting and shining into your heart a beautiful silver and golden light. Feel yourself being touched by this person's love. See the spiritual light of love on your loved one's face. See them serving you, supporting you.

Now, look at the others who played out victim or abuse energy and let the spiritual light spread to them as you say to them, "I set you free to learn your own self-empowerment and autonomy." Now, with a sword of light, cut the golden chains that have bound them to you in the role of rescuer, caretaker, or savior. Surrender them to the light of spirit to show them the way, detached from the results.

Annotated Bibliography

Atteshlis, Stylianos (better known as Daskalos). Strovolos, Cyprus, Lectures (1991–1994) on the subject of divine male/female energies. (Referenced: "On the myth of Theseus, Ariadne, and the Minotaur.")

Wonderful lectures on the heart of esoteric Christianity.

Atteshlis, Stylianos (1992). The Esoteric Teachings: A Christian Approach to Truth, the STOA series, revised English edition. (Referenced: Chapter 15, "Elementals," pp. 145–154; Chapter 5, "Archangels," pp. 59–67.)

Wonderful guidebook to spiritual healing, esoteric Christianity, and the mystical teachings of Christ.

Baba, Meher (1995). Discourses. Sheriar Press, Inc., third printing. (Referenced: pp. 399–403, "God as Infinite Love.")

Excellent reference for metaphysics and spiritual principles.

Chapman, Gary, and Ross Campbell (1997). The Five Love Languages of Children. Northfield Publishing, Chicago. (Referenced: Chapters 2–6.)

A must-read for anyone interested in parenting and partnerships.

Demetry, Nicholas C., and Edwin L. Clonts (2007). The Healing Power of Archangels: For Support and Direction in These Apocalyptic Times. Verlagsgruppe Random House. (Referenced: "Creating Virtue From Stillness," pp. 74–122.) From the original manuscript "Apocalypse of Peace" by Edwin L. Clonts and Nicholas C. Demetry (copyright 2007, Kosel-Verlag, Munchen, Germany).

A good book to prepare readers for the coming collective changes of 2012 and beyond.

Demetry, Nicholas C., and Edwin L. Clonts (2001). *Awakening Love: Universal Mission: Spiritual Healing in Psychology and Medicine.* Blue Dolphin Publishing. (Referenced: Chapters on chakras and self-limiting beliefs.)

Excellent reference on spiritually healing the personality and awakening love.

Giligan, Carol (1982). *In a Different Voice.* Harvard University Press. Included in the Integral Life Practice Publications Kit.

> *Well-researched study of psychological/social differences in men and women and how each applies to relationships, decision-making, ethics, and values. Well worth reading.*

Hayes, Patricia. RoHun Therapy Training Program at Delphi University, 1984–1986.

> *Presents basic concepts referred to in books on male–female healing, inner child work, archetypes and chakras and provides an understanding of self-limiting thought patterns and how they operate in our lives. A wonderful spiritual and psychological program that has inspired me in my own work for many years, it forms the foundation for chakra healing presented in this book. It was an honor for me to learn and to teach at Delphi University in the early years of the program's development.*

Hawkins, David R. (2002). *Power vs. Force: The Hidden Determinants of Human Behavior.* Hay House, Carlsbad, California.

> *Info on states of consciousness and life-force energy. Includes a logarithmic ranking of levels of consciousness and helpful self-testing methods.*

Hellinger, Bert (1998). *Love's Hidden Symmetry: What Makes Love Work in Relationships.* Zeig, Tucker, and Co., as presented to me by transpersonal family systems therapist Joachim Vieregge (1996–2009).

> *General principles of family dynamics and processes to reestablish healthy family roles, also relevant to ancestral healing. Being a participant, informal student, and observer of family systems work by Bert Hellinger (as practiced by Joachim Vieregge, Munchen, Germany) has inspired my own development of individual therapeutic processes for my students and patients in the last decade of my psychiatric practice.*

Jones, Marie D. (2008). *2013: Envisioning the World After the Events of 2012.* New Page Books. (Referenced: Chapter 4, p. 82.)

A good compendium of changes going on now in connection with 2012.

Klemp, Harold (2008). Hu, *The Most Beautiful Prayer.* Eckankar. (Referenced: pp. 1–65.)

A great book that describes the nature of non-directed prayer and the spiritual upliftment and healing that comes from singing the sacred sound of Hu. A CD of the Hu-song is included.

Laszlo, Ervin (2006). *The Chaos Point: The World at the Crossroads.* Inner Traditions. (Referenced: pp. 89–93.)

A great book on the new science, 2012, and shifting of global consciousness.

Laszlo, Ervin (2008). *Quantum Shift in the Global Brain: How the New Scientific Reality Can Change Us and Our World.* Inner Traditions. (Referenced: pp. 104–107.)

An excellent book merging the new sciences and consciousness research.

Reyo, Zulma (2002). *Karma and Sexuality: The Transforming Energies of Spiritual Development.* Ashgrove Publishing, London and Bath. (Referenced: Chapter 6, "Relationship Dynamics," pp. 85–100.)

Provides a good understanding of how to restore the sacredness of life-force energy and how male–female energetic polarities function in relationships.

Wauters, Ambika (1997). *Chakras and Their Archetypes.* The Crossing Press.

> *A pioneering work relating chakras and archetypes, it includes good meditations.*

Zolla, Elemire (1981). *The Androgyne Reconciliation of Male and Female.* Crossroad Publishing Company.

> *A wealth of information, stories, and historical references on androgyny and male–female alchemy.*

Resources

For Seminars, Training Programs on Spiritual Healing, Meditation, Trans-personal Psychology, books, and CDs, go to **www.etherikos.com.**

Czech Republic
Kristyna Berankova
Kristyna.berankova@gmail.com

Germany
Munich area only
Gertrand Anzenhofer
0049-89-831-924

Germany
Hartmut Suffert
hartmutsuffert@web.de

Greece
www.PatmosLight.com

Hungary
Attila Csaba
attila.csaba@etherikos.hu

Iceland
Kristinsjofn@simnet.is

Lithuania
egidijus@ignera.lt

Poland
Agnieska Gutral
poczta@fujisan.pl

Slovakia
Eva and Rudi Stark
0042-190-363-1640

USA
Margaret Ann Tufts
tufts1@gmail.com
678-740-6097

Nicholas C. Demetry, M.D.
770-435-0180

FOUR STAGES TO DIVINE LOVE

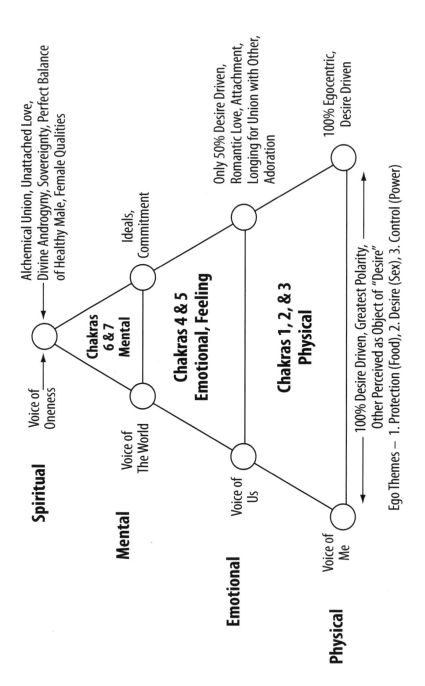

Spiritual — Voice of Oneness — Chakras 6 & 7 Mental — Alchemical Union, Unattached Love, Divine Androgyny, Sovereignty, Perfect Balance of Healthy Male, Female Qualities — Ideals, Commitment

Mental — Voice of The World — Chakras 4 & 5 Emotional, Feeling — Only 50% Desire Driven, Romantic Love, Attachment, Longing for Union with Other, Adoration

Emotional — Voice of Us — Chakras 1, 2, & 3 Physical — 100% Egocentric, Desire Driven

Physical — Voice of Me — 100% Desire Driven, Greatest Polarity, Other Perceived as Object of "Desire"

Ego Themes — 1. Protection (Food), 2. Desire (Sex), 3. Control (Power)

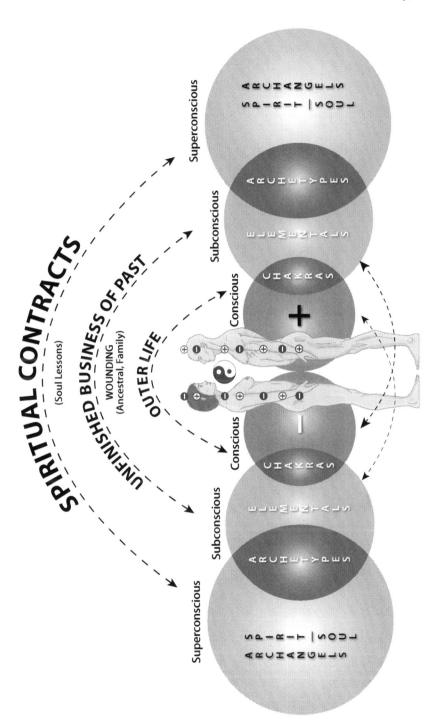

6867206R0

Made in the USA
Charleston, SC
17 December 2010